Open Mind

Elementary Workbook

Ingrid Wisniewska

Concept development:
Mariela Gil Vierma

MACMILLAN

Macmillan Education
4 Crinan Street
London N1 9XW
A division of Springer Nature Limited

Companies and representatives throughout the world

ISBN 978-0-230-45765-2 (with key)
978-0-230-45849-9 (without key)

Text, design and illustration © Springer Nature
Limited 2014
Written by Ingrid Wisniewska and Andreina España
Additional material by Angela Hewitt

This edition published 2014
First edition published 2010

Designed by emc design ltd
Illustrated by Peter Cornwell pp35, 44, 49, 54; Sally
Elford pp27, 29, 38, 46; Mo Choy Design Ltd. pp31, 40,
55; Paul Williams (Sylvie Poggio Artists) pp6, 11, 15, 19,
34, 43, 56, 59, 61, 67
Cover design by emc design ltd
Cover photographs by **Getty Images**/Reza Eastakhria,
Getty Images/Tim Robberts
Picture research by Susannah Jayes

Authors' acknowledgements
The authors would like to thank the schools, teachers
and students whose input has been invaluable in
preparing this new edition. They would also like to thank
the editorial and design teams at Macmillan for doing
such a great job of organising the material and bringing
it to life.

The publishers would like to thank the following
educators and institutions who reviewed materials and
provided us with invaluable insight and feedback for the
development of the Open Mind series:
Petra Florianová, Gymnázium, Praha 6, Arabská 14; Inés
Frigerio, Universidad Nacional de Río Cuarto; Alison
Greenwood, University of Bologna, Centro Linguistico
di Ateneo; Roumyana Yaneva Ivanova, The American
College of Sofia; Táňa Jančaříková, SOŠ Drtinova
Prague; Mari Carmen Lafuente, Escuela Oficial de
Idiomas Hospitalet, Barcelona; Alice Lockyer, Pompeu
Fabra University; Javier Roque Sandro Majul, Windmill
School of English; Paul Neale, Susan Carol Owens and
Beverley Anne Sharp, Cambridge Academy of English;
Audrey Renton, Dubai Men's College, Higher Colleges of
Technology, UAE; Martin Stanley, British Council, Bilbao;
Luiza Wójtowicz-Waga, Warsaw Study Centre; Escuela
Oficial de Idiomas de Getxo; Cámara de Comercio de
Bilbao; Universidad Autónoma de Bellaterra; Escuela
Oficial de Idiomas EOI de Barcelona; University of
Barcelona; Escuela Oficial de Idiomas Sant Gervasi.

The authors and publishers would like to thank the
following for permission to reproduce their photographs:
Alamy/Beyond Fotomedia GmbH p5(tr), Alamy/David
Burton p21(5), Alamy/BRUCE COLEMAN INC. p64(tcr),
Alamy/Tony Cordoza p21(6), Alamy/Rob Crandall p58,
Alamy/Peter Forsberg/Europe p72, Alamy/Tony French
p10(A), Alamy/Imagebroker pp14,21(3),74(tcmr), Alamy/
Evgeny Karandaev p47(4), Alamy/Kris Kelly p47(3),
Alamy/MBI pp5(tm),24, Alamy/Mark Richardson p10(B),
Alamy/Dmitry Shironosov p71(2), Alamy/M.Sobreira
p21(4), Alamy/Texas Stock Photo p42(cl), Alamy/
Val Thoermer p71(1), Alamy/Hugh Threlfall p47(2),
Alamy/Wavebreak Media ltd p13, Alamy/Steve Welsh
p10(C); **Apple Computers**/Courtesy Apple Computers
p47(1); **Bananastock** pp29(br),44(tmr); **Brand X**
pp10(E),47(5),52(8),69(cl); **ComStock** pp44(tl),52(1,4,9);
Corbis/Bettmann p68, Corbis/Erik Isakson/Blend
Images p42(cm), Corbis/Andersen Ross/Blend Images
p26, Corbis/Don Hammond/Design Pics p69(cr), Corbis/
Emmanuel Dunand/epa p64(tl), Corbis/Alan Copson/
JAI p33(tcr), Corbis/Tabor Gus p42(cr), Corbis/Hulton
Deutsch Collection p64(tcl), Corbis/Frank Sober/
Imagebroker p71(tl), Corbis/Ed Kashi p65(b), Corbis/
moodboard p69(cm), Corbis/Ocean pp23,44(tr), Corbis/
Studio Eye p60; **Getty Images** p52(7,10,13), Getty
Images/Slim Aarons p71(tm), Getty Images/Apelöga
p8, Getty Images/Gonzalo Azumendi p33(cl), Getty
Images/Michael Blann p21(7), Getty Images/zhang
bo p7, Getty Images/Greg Ceo p46(tr), Getty Images/
Emilio Ereza p21(1), Getty Images/French School
p10(F), Getty Images/Don Fuchs p74(t), Getty Images/
Fuse pp5(tcr),44(tml), Getty Images/Rubberball/Mike
Kemp p41, Getty Images/Christian Kober p28, Getty
Images/Michael Krinke p71(3), Getty Images/Siegfried
Layda p33(tcl), Getty Images/Lonely Planet p33(cm),
Getty Images/Roy Mehta p16(tr), Getty Images/Moment
p46(tmr), Getty Images/Jose Luis Pelaez Inc p4, Getty
Images/Medioimages/Photodisc p9, Getty Images/
Roberto A Sanchez p16(tmr), Getty Images/Andrew
Unangst p47(cr), Getty Images/Design Pics/Sean White
p74(cr); **Macmillan Publishers Ltd**/Paul Bricknell
p52(6), Macmillan Publishers Ltd/Rob Judges/Des
Dubber p10(D), Macmillan Publishers Ltd/David Tolley/
Dean Ryan p30, Macmillan Publishers Ltd/David Tolley
p52(5); **PHOTOALTO** p57; **Photodisc** p17, Photodisc/
Getty Images p52(3); **Photoshot**/Kenneth W. Fink
p33(tcm), Photoshot/NHPA p65(tr); **Press Association
Images**/Steve Parsons/PA Archive p64(cl); **Rex
Features**/Tom Dymond p64(cr), Rex Features/©Sony
Pics/Everett p75(cr), Rex Features/©Warner Br/
Everett p73, Rex Features/©Weinstein/Everett p75(tr),
Rex Features/ITV p64(tr), Rex Features/RESO p12,
Rex Features/Snap Stills p75(br); **Superstock**/i love
images p18; **Thinkstock**/Hemera p52(11), Thinkstock/
Istockphoto pp21(2),32,36,47(c),50, Thinkstock/George
Doyle/Stockbyte p52(2); **Up the Resolution** p52(12).

Printed and bound by Ashford Colour Press Ltd.

2019
10 9 8

CONTENTS

AUDIOSCRIPT
page 76

ANSWER KEY
page 81

UNIT 1 NICE TO MEET YOU!

1 READING: recognising cognates

A Read the text. Underline the cognates.

My name is Hilda Gonzalez. I'm a student at Bristol University.
I study English and medicine. I have a part-time job in a pharmacy.
My interests are literature, music, films and badminton. I love animals,
especially horses. My best friend is Ayako Kubota. We are in the same
English class. Our teacher is Mr Mason.

B Match the words from the text to the correct meaning.

1	English	a)	a type of sport
2	medicine	b)	a type of animal
3	university	c)	a language
4	badminton	d)	an academic subject
5	horse	e)	a group of students
6	class	f)	a place of study

C Write four more English words that are cognates in your language.

1 _____   3 _____

2 _____   4 _____

2 VOCABULARY: useful questions

**A))) 01 Complete the questions with the words from the box.
Then listen and check your answers.**

help   mean   repeat   say   speak   ~~spell~~

1 Can you *spell* that?
2 Can you _____ more slowly?
3 How do you _____ that in English?
4 Can you _____ that, please?
5 What does that _____?
6 Can you _____ me?

B Complete the conversations with the questions from Exercise A.

1 A: My name is Elvira.
   B: _____
   A: Sure. It's E-L-V-I-R-A.
   B: Thank you.

2 A: Open your books to page 24.
   B: _____
   A: Yes. Open your books to page 24.

3 A: 'Excellent'? _____
   B: It means 'very good'!

4 A: Hi, my name's Hiroyoshi.
   B: _____
   A: My name is … Hi … ro … yo … shi.

5 A: _____
   B: It's 'birthday' in English.

6 A: I don't understand the homework.
      _____
   B: Yes, of course.

3 GRAMMAR: *be* — statements and *Yes/No* questions

A Choose the correct option to complete the sentences.

1 Sebastian is / am / are from Poland.
2 Is / Are / Am they university students?
3 Jim isn't / aren't from New York City.
4 Is / Am / Are they English students?
5 I am / is / are from Hong Kong.
6 Rio de Janeiro is / are / am a big city.

B Read the information. Complete the sentences.

> **student card**
>
> Name: Kate
> Age: 19
> City and country: Newbury, UK
> Studies: Business

> **student card**
>
> Name: Hiro
> Age: 23
> City and country: Nagoya, Japan
> Studies: Business

> **student card**
>
> Name: Rafael
> Age: 31
> City and country: Recife, Brazil
> Studies: Music

1 Hiro _____ 23 years old.
2 Kate _____ from Brazil.
3 Rafael: I _____ 31 years old.
4 Kate and Hiro: We _____ business students.
5 Kate: _____ Hiro from the UK?
   Rafael: No, he _____.
6 A: _____ Hiro and Kate business students?
   B: Yes, they _____.
7 Rafael: _____ you from Japan?
   Kate: No, I _____.
8 Rafael: _____ you music students?
   Kate and Hiro: No, we _____.
9 Hiro: Is Kate 19?
   Rafael: Yes, she _____.

WHAT'S RIGHT?

(✗) She has 25 years.
(✓) _____

C Complete the conversation between Kate and Hiro. Use short forms where possible.

Kate: Hi. I (1) _____ Kate. I (2) _____ from the UK.
Hiro: My name (3) _____ Hiro. I (4) _____ from Nagoya.
       It (5) _____ in Japan. (6) _____ you from London?
Kate: No, I (7) _____ from London. I (8) _____ from Newbury.
Hiro: (9) _____ it a big city?
Kate: No, it (10) _____. It (11) _____ a small town.
       (12) _____ you a business student?
Hiro: Yes, I (13) _____. We (14) _____ in the same class!

4 COMMUNICATION STRATEGY: using polite language

A 🎧 02 **Complete the conversation with the phrases from the box. Then listen and check your answers.**

Thanks   You're welcome   Excuse me   Thank you   please

Receptionist: (1) _____, can you spell your surname, (2) _____?
Ms Cardoza: Yes, it's C-A-R-D-O-Z-A.
Receptionist: (3) _____. And what's your phone number?
Ms Cardoza: It's 01743 214091.
Receptionist: OK. You're in room 235. Here's your room key.
Ms Cardoza: (4) _____.
Receptionist: (5) _____. Enjoy your stay.

B **Look at the pictures. Complete the conversations with polite phrases from Exercise A.**

(1) _____, where is the university?

Could you fill in this form, (2) _____?

Thank you.

(3) _____.

5 VOCABULARY: ordinal numbers

A 🎧 03 Listen and write the ordinal numbers you hear. Write the numbers in the first column.

1	9th	ninth
2		
3		
4		
5		
6		

B Now write each number in words in the second column.

C Read the sentences. Write the words in **bold** in numbers.

1 This Saturday is the **twenty-seventh**. _____
2 My next class is on the **eleventh**. _____
3 My birthday is on the **thirteenth** of August. _____
4 Today is September the **twenty-second**. _____
5 US Independence Day is on the **fourth** of July. _____
6 The last day of June is the **thirtieth**. _____

6 GRAMMAR: be – information questions

A Complete the questions with the correct question word from the box.

How   What   When   Where

1 _____ are you from?   3 _____ old are you?
2 _____ is your name?   4 _____ is your birthday?

B 🎧 04 Listen to the voicemail message and complete the form.

First name:	
Surname:	
Country:	
Age:	
Telephone number:	

C Complete the questions and answers about the woman from Exercise B. Use questions from Exercise A in the correct form.

1 A: _____ her first name?
   B: Her first name is _____.
2 A: _____
   B: Her surname is _____.
3 A: _____
   B: She's from _____.
4 A: _____
   B: She is _____ years old.
5 A: _____ her phone number?
   B: It's _____.

WHAT'S RIGHT?
❌ Where you are from?
✓ _____

Listen and write

A **05** Listen to the conversation. Complete the online form with the information.

First name:

Surname:

Age:

Birthday:

Email:

jane192@mail.com

B Complete the form with your information.

First name:

Birthday:

Surname:

Email:

Age:

Over to You

C Use the information in the form in Exercise B to write a paragraph about yourself.

My first name's …

WRITING TUTOR

My name is … / I'm …
My … is on …
My … is …

A Find the ordinal numbers in the word search and write them below. The words can go forwards (→), down (↓) or diagonally (↗).

S	E	V	E	N	T	E	E	N	T	H
F	I	R	S	T	L	W	Y	N	V	F
S	C	T	M	N	X	Y	L	Q	H	T
F	E	H	N	D	D	D	X	T	T	N
O	T	V	R	G	N	B	N	E	W	T
U	F	M	E	O	V	E	C	N	P	P
R	L	I	C	N	E	W	L	T	K	D
T	B	E	F	T	T	J	Y	H	R	T
H	S	B	F	T	P	H	C	I	M	K
F	R	I	M	W	H	K	H	P	C	L
Q	F	J	K	K	F	T	B	N	N	L

5th 15th 1st 4th 2nd 17th 7th 10th 3rd

_____   _____
_____   _____
_____   _____
_____

B Complete the sentences with the missing word. Which are the letters in the circles?

1 Lucia ◯ __ from Brazil.

2 August is the __ __ ◯ __ __ __ month of the year.

3 Can you __ __ ◯ __ __ more slowly?

4 Can you ◯ __ __ __ me?

5 How __ ◯ __ are you?

6 What does this __ __ __ ◯ ?

7 Can you ◯ __ __ __ __ that?

Letters in circles: 1 __ 2 __ 3 __ 4 __ 5 __ 6 __ 7 __

C Now rearrange the circled letters. What's the new word?

_____

D Decode the conversation. The numbers correspond to the letters in the alphabet.

A: 23-8-5-18-5 1-18-5 25-15-21 6-18-15-13?
B: 9'-13 6-18-15-13 13-1-4-18-9-4. 1-14-4 25-15-21?
A: 9'-13 6-18-15-13 18-15-13-5. 13-25 14-1-13-5'-19 16-1-15-12-15.
B: 14-9-3-5 20-15 13-5-5-20 25-15-21. 9'-13 19-15-14-9-1.
A: Where _____?
B: _____
A: _____
B: _____

UNIT 2 WHAT DO YOU DO?

1 VOCABULARY: occupations

A Rearrange the letters and match the occupations to the correct photo.

1 otrcdo _____
2 eirfifhegtr _____
3 atxi eridvr _____

4 nnergeie _____
5 ilcpeo rficofe _____
6 rtiwre _____

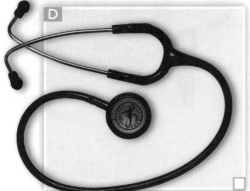

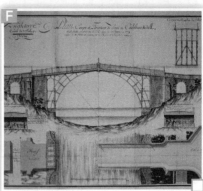

B 》06 Listen to Teresa. What is her opinion about these occupations? Number the occupations, according to her opinion, from interesting (1) to not interesting (6).

☐ engineer
☐ police officer
☐ doctor
☐ firefighter
☐ writer
☐ taxi driver

2 GRAMMAR: articles

A Decide if the words in the box use *a*, *an* or – (no article). Write them in the table.

actor artist engineer lawyers musician
singer students teacher writers

a	*an*	–

B Choose the correct option to complete the sentences.

1 My sister is a / (an) / the / – engineer.
2 London is a / an / the / – capital of England.
3 My brothers are a / an / the / – actors.
4 Our band is on a / an / the / – internet.
5 We're a / an / the / – actors in a TV show. A / An / The / – show is on Mondays.

C There is one mistake in each sentence. Rewrite the sentences correctly.

1 Are you teacher? _____
2 They are a doctors in the health service. _____
3 My brother is a doctors. _____
4 Is Dave an lawyer? _____
5 I am not student. _____
6 My brother is teacher in a school. A school is in Brighton. _____

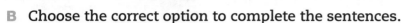

WHAT'S RIGHT?

(X) He is musician.

(✓) _____

3 VOCABULARY: family members

A 🔊 07 Listen to Angela describing her family. Write the names from the box in the correct places.

Emma Frank Kate Leo Lucy Mary Mike Sheila

1 _____

2 _____   3 _____

4 _____   5 _____   6 _____   Angela

7 _____   8 _____

B Use the family tree in Exercise A to complete the sentences.

Angela: Mary is my (1) _____. Sheila and Frank are my
(2) _____. Mike is my (3) _____. Kate is
my (4) _____. (5) _____ is her husband.
(6) _____ and (7) _____ are their daughters.
Sheila and Frank are their (8) _____.

A Read the sentences about Brenda. Match each sentence to the missing information. Write the correct letter in the box.

1 Brenda _____ is a lawyer. ☐
2 She lives in _____. ☐
3 Brenda starts work at _____. ☐
4 She thinks her job is very _____. ☐
5 Her husband is an _____. ☐
6 Their _____ is a student. ☐

a) an adjective   d) a time
b) a place   e) an occupation
c) a surname   f) a family member

B 🔊 08 Listen and complete the sentences (1–6) in Exercise A. Were your predictions correct?

5 GRAMMAR: possession

A Complete the sentences with the correct form of *have got*. Use contractions.

Gina	✓ brother	✗ sister
Tom	✗ brother	✓ sister
Andy and Pete	✗ laptop	✓ bicycle
Me	✓ laptop	✗ bicycle

1 Gina _____ _____ a brother, but she _____ _____ a sister.
2 Tom _____ _____ a brother, but he _____ _____ a sister.
3 Andy and Pete _____ _____ laptops, but they _____ _____ bicycles.
4 I _____ _____ a laptop, but I _____ _____ a bicycle.

B Complete the sentences with the possessive form of the words in brackets.

1 Her _____ (*sister*) husband is a doctor.
2 Our _____ (*children*) teacher is from England.
3 _____ (*Tom*) parents live in Santiago.
4 My _____ (*mother*) best friend is from Italy.
5 His _____ (*grandparents*) house is near the school.
6 Your _____ (*parents*) jobs are very exciting.

WHAT'S RIGHT?

✗ My cats name is Tippy.

✓ _____

C Complete the sentences with the correct possessive pronoun.

1 Her name isn't Alexa. Alexa is my name. _____ is Tania.
2 She hasn't got a red bicycle. I've got a red bicycle. This bicycle is _____.
3 They live in a big house. This is their house. This house is _____.
4 Our classroom is 5A. Your classroom is 6B. Classroom 5A is _____, and classroom 6B is _____.
5 Rachel is a teacher, and Bob is a firefighter. Her job isn't dangerous, but _____ is very dangerous.
6 She has green eyes, and he has blue eyes. _____ are green, and _____ are blue.

6 WRITING: understanding the mechanics

A There is one mistake with capital letters in each of the sentences. Find the mistake and match it to a rule. Then correct the mistakes.

1 My birthday is in ᴺnovember.	a) languages
2 We are from peru.	b) countries
3 They study english.	c) names of people
4 My sister and i are doctors.	d) towns and cities
5 My teacher is Mr daniels.	e) days of the week
6 it is five o'clock.	f) months
7 Antonia lives in rome.	g) the word *I*
8 Your class is on wednesday.	h) the beginning of a sentence

B Read the paragraph. Make six sentences. Add full stops at the end of the sentences and capital letters at the beginning of the sentences.

my sister Alison is a writer she writes short stories and books for children her job is very interesting, but it is also difficult she sometimes travels around the country and talks about her work her books are very popular with children and adults she's got two awards for best children's books of the year

1 _____

2 _____

3 _____

4 _____

5 _____

6 _____

Read and write

A Read about Max Garcia's life. What is his job?

Max Garcia **is my cousin. He's 33 and he's a sound engineer.** He's from the USA but he lives in London. He speaks French and Spanish. He loves his job because he listens to great bands from all over the world and he meets famous musicians.

Max has got a big family. His two brothers live in Miami, and his sister lives in Madrid. Max's dad, Alan, is a police officer, and his mum is a piano teacher. Max visits his family twice a year.

B Read the article again and answer the questions.

1 How old is Max?
_____

2 Is he happy about his job? Why?
_____

3 Is Max's family small?
_____

4 What's his dad's name?
_____

5 What's his mum's job?
_____

C Write the types of information in the order they appear in the article. Check your answers. Then make notes about one of your family members next to each type of information.

Family   Job   Other information   ~~Name~~   Relationship
Lives   Age   Opinion about job   Nationality

	Types of information	Notes about your family
1	Name	
2		
3		
4		
5		
6		
7		
8		
9		

Over to You

D ✎ In your notebook, write a paragraph about your family member. Use your notes in Exercise C and the text in Exercise A to help you.

WRITING TUTOR

(name) *is my …*
He/She is a/an…
He/She is from / lives in …
He/She loves/likes his/her job because …
He/She has a big/small family.

DOWN TIME

A **Read the text about Emma's family. Answer the question and write the names of the people under the correct picture.**

Hi! I'm Emma. I've got two brothers and a sister. My mum's name is Brenda, and my dad's name is Mike. My dad's dad is Edward, and his wife is Annette. My mum's dad is Richard, and my mum's mum is Eleanor. My mum's got a sister. Her name's Lauren. My sister's name is Susan, and her husband's name is Sam. They have two children, Sara and Sophie. I've also got two brothers: Rick and Andrew. Rick is married to Clare. They have a daughter. Her name is Naomi. My other brother, Andrew, hasn't got kids. Oh, and my husband's name is Tim.

Who are Edward, Annette, Eleanor and Richard? Emma's _____

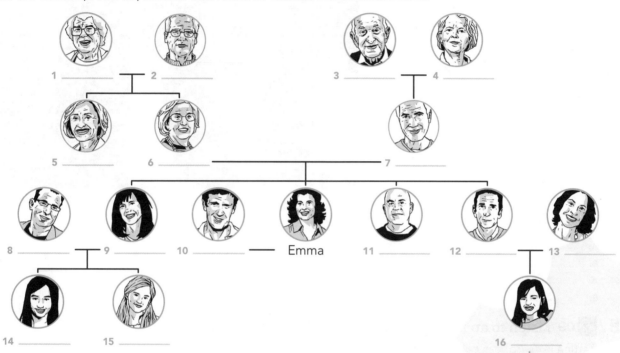

1 _____   2 _____   3 _____   4 _____

5 _____   6 _____   7 _____

8 _____   9 _____   10 _____   Emma   11 _____   12 _____   13 _____

14 _____   15 _____   16 _____

B **Find the jobs. Separate the words with a line and write them underneath.**

singersoftwareengineerlawyerartistfirefighterpoliceofficersoldiertaxidriverarchitectjournalistdoctor

_____

C **Match the two halves.**

| well | interesting | | salary | -paid | work |

| good | hard | job | | -working | security |

UNIT 3 DOWN TIME

1 GRAMMAR: present simple — statements and *Yes/No* questions

A Read the information about Rose and Kevin. Complete the sentences.

What do you do in your free time?

	Rose	Kevin
listen to music	✓	✓
read magazines	✗	✗
watch TV	✗	✓
play the guitar	✗	✓
buy CDs	✓	✓

Rose

Kevin

1 Kevin _____ to music.
2 Rose _____ TV and
   she _____ magazines.
3 A: _____ Rose _____ the guitar?
   B: _____, she _____ .
4 A: _____ Rose and Kevin _____ CDs?
   B: _____, they _____ .
5 A: _____ Kevin _____ magazines?
   B: _____, he _____ .

B 🎧 09 Listen to an interview and choose the correct option.

1 Bettina likes / doesn't like folk music.
2 She plays / doesn't play the guitar.
3 Bettina's parents listen / don't listen to music a lot.
4 She buys / doesn't buy MP3s online.

C 🎧 09 Complete the interview. Then listen again and check your answers.

A: Hi, Bettina. Can I ask you some questions for a survey?
B: Sure! Go ahead.
A: (1) _____ to music?
B: Yes, I do. I listen to folk music. I really like folk music.
A: And (2) _____ the guitar?
B: No, I don't.
A: (3) _____ to music a lot?
B: No, they don't.
A: (4) _____ a lot of CDs?
B: No, I don't. I (5) _____ MP3s online.
A: Great! That's all. Thanks a lot!
B: Sure, no problem.

WHAT'S RIGHT?

✗ Does he read books? Yes, he reads.

✓ _____

16

2 READING: recognising cognates

A Read the text and (circle) the cognates.
These words will help you understand the text.

DO YOU LIKE TO READ BOOKS?

Share your opinions about your favourite books here.

I like mystery stories. I have a big collection of Agatha Christie books. I love puzzles and I always try to find the solution before the end! Miss Marple and Sherlock Holmes are my favourite detectives. – Suzie

I like fantasy novels — especially when there is a series of books with the same characters. My favourite is *A Song of Ice and Fire*. I imagine I'm one of the people in the book! – Danni

I only read biographies and historical books. I want to read about real events and real people. I don't like fantasies or romantic novels. – Leo

I love a good romantic story. I can live in a fantasy world for a short time. And there is always a happy ending. – Monika

B Answer these questions about the text in Exercise A.

1 Who doesn't like fiction? _____
2 Who likes to read more than one book about one story? _____
3 Who likes true stories about people? _____
4 Who likes love stories? _____
5 Who has a lot of books by the same author? _____ and
_____

3 VOCABULARY: free-time activities

A Match the verbs to the nouns to make free-time activities.

1 play   a) TV
2 do   b) video games
3 listen to   c) friends
4 go   d) the cinema
5 play   e) music
6 go to   f) bowling
7 see   g) exercise
8 watch   h) sport

B Complete the sentences with six of the phrases from Exercise A.

1 I often _____ with my friends in the evening. I love science-fiction films.
2 Marty likes to _____ at the weekend. He loves football and basketball.
3 I like to be in good shape so I usually _____ in the gym twice a week. I use the weights and the treadmill.
4 We usually _____ on Saturday nights. It's not a difficult sport to play and it's a good way to meet people.
5 Henry likes to _____ in the evening. He has a big collection of CDs.
6 John likes to _____ at night. He likes documentaries and quiz shows.

4 GRAMMAR: present simple – information questions

A Match the questions to the answers.

1 When do Bob and Jerry go bowling?
2 What do Sally and Paula do on Friday nights?
3 Where does Jane usually play tennis?
4 Where do you do your homework?
5 Where does your brother buy music?
6 Who does Linda play tennis with?

a) Her sister.
b) In the park.
c) Online.
d) At the weekend.
e) They eat out.
f) At home.

B Read the survey about websites. Complete the questions with *What*, *Where*, *When*, *Why* or *Who*. Then complete the survey.

Internet Survey

1 *What* websites do you visit every day?

[   ]

2 _____ do you like them?

[   ]

3 _____ do you visit them?

○ in the morning ○ during the day ○ at night

4 _____ do you talk about them with?

[   ]

5 _____ do you use the internet?

○ at home ○ at work ○ at university ○ in the library

C Read the text about Tony. Then read the answers and write the questions.

WHAT'S RIGHT?

(✗) What he does in his free time?

(✓) _____

Tony likes to play football in his free time. He plays with his old school friends. They usually play on Saturday afternoons in the park near his home. He likes football because it's a very good sport – relaxing, healthy and fun.

1 *What does Tony like to do in his free time?* — He likes to play football.
2 _____ — With his old school friends.
3 _____ — On Saturday afternoons.
4 _____ — In the park near his home.
5 _____ — Because it's relaxing, healthy and fun.

5 COMMUNICATION STRATEGY: asking for opinions

Complete the questions with the phrases from the box. Then match to the best answer.

Do you   How about   What do you   What's your

1   I don't like video games. They're too violent.
_____ think?

2   I play football and tennis. _____ you?

3   I don't like classical music. _____ opinion?

4   This new science-fiction film is great.
_____ agree?

a)   I prefer hip-hop.
b)   Yes, I do.
c)   I don't play sport.
d)   I'm not sure. They're OK sometimes.

6 VOCABULARY: personality adjectives

A   🎧 10 Listen and write the correct adjectives from the box under each picture.

considerate   funny   loyal   popular   shy   sociable

1   Marisa: _____

2   Lucy: _____

3   Eddie: _____

4   Simon: _____

5   Clare: _____

6   Andy: _____

B   Choose the correct option to complete the letter.

Dear Wendy,

I don't have many friends. I'm very **(1)** popular / shy. I sometimes go to parties, but I'm not very **(2)** confident / loyal and I don't talk to anyone. My best friend is Amy. She has a lot of friends. She is very **(3)** independent / popular, and her stories are very **(4)** funny / considerate. She's an **(5)** introvert / extrovert. Amy introduces me to new people because she is a very **(6)** shy / loyal friend. But I'm an **(7)** extrovert / introvert and I'm not **(8)** sociable / shy. Please help me.

Yours,

Janet

Listen and write

A 🔊 11 Listen to the radio show and tick (✓) the kinds of things the guests mention.

- ☐ their personality
- ☐ their daily activities
- ☐ their family
- ☐ their free-time activities
- ☐ their friends

B 🔊 11 Listen to the radio show again and write the person's initial next to the personality adjective. Write A for Alex, J for Jenny or A/J for both.

1 shy _____   2 sociable _____   3 popular _____   4 funny _____

Then note the daily or free-time activities they like.

write new songs _____   watch a film _____
go bowling _____   do exercise at the gym _____
see friends _____   practise the guitar _____
go to parties _____

C Read the short descriptions. Complete the text with the adjectives from the box.

confident   considerate   funny   independent   loyal   popular   shy   sociable

a   My name's Linda. I'm very (1) _____. I like going to parties and seeing my friends at the weekend. I'm also quite (2) _____, and feel comfortable with new people and in new situations. I'm very (3) _____ and like to do things my own way.

b   My name's Mark. I have lots of friends and I am quite (4) _____. I can also be (5) _____ and I like to tell jokes. I enjoy playing video games with my friends.

c   My name's Carla. I'm quite (6) _____ when I meet new people, but I have some very good and (7) _____ friends who are always there for me when I need them. I am very (8) _____ and I'm always there for my friends.

Over to You

D Now make notes to complete the table with information about yourself. What are you like? What are your daily activities? What are your free-time activities?

Personality	Daily activities	Free-time activities

WRITING TUTOR

I'm very/quite …
I like/enjoy (going/playing, etc) …

E ✎ Now write three sentences about you. Write one sentence about your personality, one about your daily activities and one about your free-time activities. Use your notes from Exercise D.

_____
_____
_____

DOWN TIME

A Write the phrases from the box under the correct photo.

go bowling   go online   go to the cinema   listen to music
play tennis   play video games   watch TV

1 _____

2 _____

3 _____

4 _____

5 _____

6 _____

7 _____

B Read the clues and complete the crossword.

1 Someone who tells jokes and is good at it is …
2 Someone who likes to meet new people is …
3 Someone who is not nervous is …
4 Someone who doesn't talk to people is …
5 Someone with lots of friends is …
6 People you like and see in your free time are your …
7 People who like parties and talk a lot are …
8 People who listen rather than talk and like quiet evenings at home are …

UNIT 4 DAY IN, DAY OUT

1 VOCABULARY: telling the time

A »🔊 12 What time is it? Listen and draw the times on the clocks.

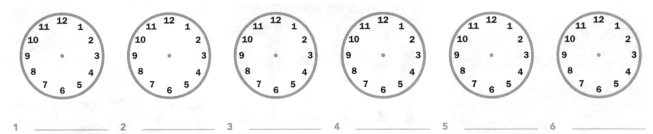

1 _____ 2 _____ 3 _____ 4 _____ 5 _____ 6 _____

B Write the time in words under each clock.

2 GRAMMAR: adverbs of frequency and adverbial phrases

A Number the frequency words in order from high (100% = 1) to low (0% = 6).

☐ sometimes ☐ often ☐ rarely ☐ usually ☐ never ☐ always

B Put the words in the correct order to form sentences.

1 always / at home / are / We / in the evening
_____

2 once a week / have dinner in a restaurant / Frank and Emilia
_____

3 Yolanda / watches / TV / rarely
_____

4 My brother / online / often / in the morning / is
_____

5 any free time / has / never / Hector
_____

6 three times a week / Clare / drives to work
_____

> **WHAT'S RIGHT?**
>
> ✗ He never is late.
>
> ✓ _____

C Rewrite the sentences with the correct adverb of frequency from the box.

~~always~~ (x 2)   sometimes   never   rarely   often   usually

1 Suzanna takes the bus every day.
Suzanna *always takes the bus*.

2 Frank and Liz go to the cinema twice a week.
Frank and Liz _____.

3 Matt goes swimming every day in his lunch break.
_____

4 Marie eats in a restaurant once a year.
_____

5 We drive to work four times a week.
_____

6 Leona is absent about once a month.
_____

7 Toby doesn't get up early on Sundays.
_____

3 LISTENING: listening for specific information

A))) 13 **Listen to Sarah describing her week. Match the days of the week to the activities.**

1	Mondays	a)	look after my sister's children
2	Tuesdays	b)	go to the design studio
3	Wednesdays	c)	invite my friends for dinner
4	Thursdays	d)	do exercise in the gym
5	Fridays	e)	ride my bike
6	Saturdays	f)	go shopping
7	Sundays	g)	go dancing

B))) 14 **Listen to Francisco describing his week. Underline the mistakes in the text.**

Hi. My name is Francisco. I'm a computer programmer. On Mondays, I usually stay at home and work online. The rest of the week I work at home. On Tuesday mornings, I do exercise in the gym. On Wednesday evenings, I go to my friend's house. On Thursday evenings, I usually stay at home. On Friday evenings, I go shopping. On Saturdays, I go to the cinema and on Sundays, I stay at home.

C))) 14 **Listen again and correct the mistakes in Exercise B.**

4 VOCABULARY: prepositions of time

A Complete the table with the words from the box.

four o'clock   midnight   night   the afternoon   the evening
the morning   the weekend   Wednesday   weekdays

on	*at*	*in*

B Complete the sentences with the correct preposition.

1 Ben usually goes shopping _____ Fridays.
2 I usually read the newspaper _____ the morning.
3 My favourite show starts _____ 6pm.
4 We sometimes watch TV _____ the evening.
5 Pete and Sally often go out _____ the weekend.
6 Pete goes to school _____ weekdays.

C Read about Mateo's daily routine. Put the events in the correct order on the timeline.

Mateo gets up at 6am. He has a shower before breakfast, and after breakfast he reads the newspaper. He goes to work at 7.30. Mateo works until 12.30pm and then he goes to the park for his lunch break. After lunch, he reads the newspaper again and then he goes to the shop to buy some food for his dinner. Then, at 1.30pm, he goes back to the office. Mateo finishes work at six o'clock. After work, he goes home and has dinner. Before dinner, he watches the news on TV. After dinner, he reads a book and goes to bed at 10.30pm.

He gets up.

He eats breakfast.

He goes to work.

He goes to the park.

He goes back to the office.

He finishes work.

He has dinner.

He goes to bed.

5 GRAMMAR: clauses with *until*, *before*, *after*

A Read the sentences and choose the correct order of events.

1 Before she comes home from school, Bella plays tennis with her friends.
   a) First, she plays tennis. Second, she comes home.
   b) First, she comes home. Second, she plays tennis.
2 After we go to the gym, we have breakfast.
   a) First, we go to the gym. Second, we have breakfast.
   b) First, we have breakfast. Second, we go to the gym.
3 Antonio has dinner before he goes home.
   a) First, he goes home. Second, he has dinner.
   b) First, he has dinner. Second, he goes home.
4 I go to the library after I go shopping.
   a) First, I go to the library. Second, I go shopping.
   b) First, I go shopping. Second, I go to the library.

B Join the two sentences. Use *before*, *after* or *until*. Remember to use the correct punctuation.

1 We go shopping. Then we go to the cinema.
   We _____. (*after*)
2 Danny goes to the library. Then he goes to his English class.
   Danny _____. (*before*)
3 My children watch TV. They stop when we have dinner.
   My _____. (*until*)
4 I practise the piano. I stop when it is eight o'clock.
   I _____. (*until*)
5 Zach and Mina cook dinner. Then they watch TV.
   After _____.
6 Becky goes to the gym. Then she has lunch.
   Before _____.

WHAT'S RIGHT?
(✗) He has a shower after has breakfast.

(✓) _____

6 WRITING: understanding the mechanics

A Read the sentences. <u>Underline</u> the subject and circle the verb in each sentence.

1 Toshihiko starts work at seven thirty.
2 It is sunny and warm today.
3 Emil and Renata go to the gym on Saturdays.
4 My brother has a very interesting job. He is a travel writer.
5 We buy music online. We rarely buy CDs from a shop.
6 It's five o'clock.

B Read the paragraph. The three words in the box are missing from the text. Put them in the correct places.

| goes | he | it |

Adam usually finishes work at 5.30pm. After work, goes to his English class. His class finishes at 7pm. Before he home, he goes to a café with his friends. Adam gets home at around 8.30pm. After dinner, he does his homework until is time to go to sleep.

Read and write

A Read this blog entry and <u>underline</u> the adverbs of frequency.

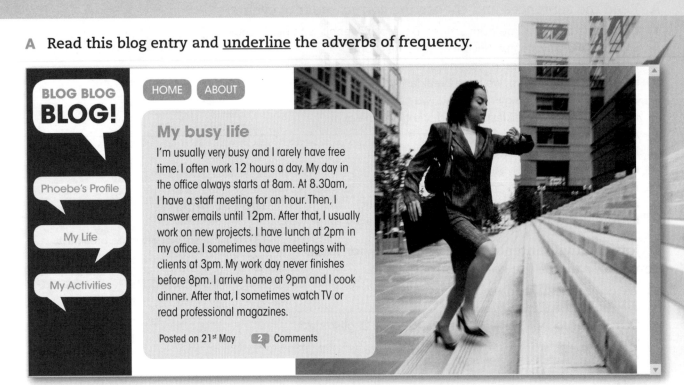

BLOG BLOG BLOG!

HOME   ABOUT

Phoebe's Profile

My Life

My Activities

My busy life

I'm usually very busy and I rarely have free time. I often work 12 hours a day. My day in the office always starts at 8am. At 8.30am, I have a staff meeting for an hour. Then, I answer emails until 12pm. After that, I usually work on new projects. I have lunch at 2pm in my office. I sometimes have meetings with clients at 3pm. My work day never finishes before 8pm. I arrive home at 9pm and I cook dinner. After that, I sometimes watch TV or read professional magazines.

Posted on 21ˢᵗ May   2 Comments

B Make a list of the activities Phoebe does during the day in the order they happen.

8am – Phoebe starts work.
8.30 –

Over to You

C Make a list of the activities you do during the day.

_____
_____
_____
_____
_____
_____

D 🖊 In your notebook, write a blog about your day, similar to the one in Exercise A. Use your list in Exercise C to help you. Remember to use adverbs of frequency and sequence words to organise your ideas in a logical way.

DOWN TIME

A Read the clues and complete the crossword.

Across

1 Someone who likes going out and meeting people is …
2 every day
3 not interesting
4 a form of exercise – sometimes I take my dog (four words)
5 almost never

Down

1 half an hour before two o'clock (two words)
2 a place to chat
3 article before a vowel
4 My favourite day is at the weekend.
5 midday
6 This fan always watches and supports his team.
7 an earlier time
8 I do this from Monday to Friday.

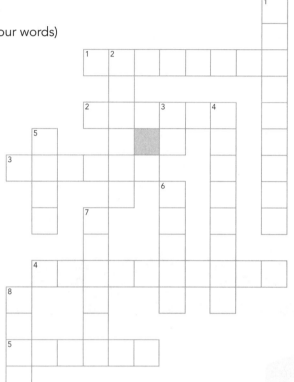

B Complete the sayings. Use the picture to help you. What word does each part of the picture represent?

1 Time waits _____ no _____.
2 Time _____ when you are having fun.
3 The early _____ catches the _____.

UNIT 5 HERE, THERE AND EVERYWHERE

1 GRAMMAR: *there is / there are* with *some, any, several, a lot of, many*

A Complete the paragraph. Use the affirmative or negative form of *be*.

Sydney, Australia is a fantastic place to visit for New Year. Every year there (1) _____ a huge celebration on New Year's Eve. There (2) _____ a lot of events all over the city: music, fireworks, parades, picnics. There (3) _____ a huge fireworks display near Sydney Harbour starting at 9pm. Arrive early because it's often difficult to find a good place to watch the fireworks. Don't forget to book a hotel in advance because there (4) _____ usually any hotel rooms left on New Year's Eve. About one million people come to Sydney for New Year. There (5) _____ many cities that have a more exciting New Year's Eve party! Come to Sydney and have a great New Year!

B Choose the correct option to complete the sentences.

1 There isn't / aren't a lot of festivals in my home town.
2 There is / are a big celebration in the UK on 5th November.
3 Is / Are there any tickets for the parade?
4 There aren't some / many music festivals here in December.
5 There aren't any / some tickets for the concert.
6 Is / Are there usually a lot of people at this festival?
7 There are any / several famous musicians in the concert.
8 There is / are a lot of visitors in the summer.

WHAT'S RIGHT?

(X) There is a lot of festivals.

(✓) _____

2 VOCABULARY: places and attractions in a city

A Write the words from the box next to the correct definition.

| art gallery   cinema   museum   park   shopping centre   zoo |

1 You watch films here. _____
2 You see old and historic objects here. _____
3 You buy clothes and toys here. _____
4 You see paintings and pictures here. _____
5 You go for a walk here. _____
6 You see interesting animals here. _____

B 🎧 15 Listen and tick (✓) the places the two friends plan to visit.

☐ art gallery ☐ café
☐ cinema ☐ shopping centre
☐ park ☐ museum
☐ zoo

C Write the names of the places from the box under each poster.

bus station   chocolate factory   cinema   shopping centre

1 _____   2 _____   3 _____   4 _____

3 READING: for the main idea

A Read the three blog entries. Match each entry to its topic.

Blog 1   a) a hotel
Blog 2   b) a restaurant
Blog 3   c) a park

B Is each blog in Exercise A positive or negative? Choose the correct option. Then <u>underline</u> the key words and phrases that helped you decide.

Tips for Tourists *Best places to stay at, eat out and visit in Miami*

| HOME | FLIGHTS | HOTELS | RESTAURANTS | THINGS TO DO | ADVICE |

1 **Parrot Jungle Island** is amazing. The gardens are beautiful, and there are thousands of exotic animals and plants. There's lots of stuff to do – take photos, watch the animal shows or relax on the private beach. It's in the heart of Miami, and there's a good bus service. A fantastic day out for the whole family.

2 **The Casa Bella** is great! Real luxury! The rooms are large and comfortable. There's a bar right next to the pool with beautiful palm trees and umbrellas. The service is excellent. And it's five minutes from the beach!

3 Don't go to **Miami Grill!** There isn't any seating outside, and inside it's too hot and not very clean. The service is terrible – the waiters are not helpful. The food isn't great, and the drinks are too expensive.

Blog 1: positive / negative
Blog 2: positive / negative
Blog 3: positive / negative

4 GRAMMAR: the imperative

A   Read the conversation. Underline all the imperative forms.

Richard: Excuse me. How do I get to the underground station?

Amelia: Go straight ahead and take the second right onto Oxford Street. Then turn left onto Green Avenue and walk for about 200 metres. Don't cross the street. The underground station is there on the left. Don't worry. It's easy to find!

Richard: Thank you very much.

**B   Complete the webpage with the words from the box.
Use the affirmative or negative imperative form.**

drink   eat   forget   give   go   have   stay   take   visit   walk

New York City

I want to go to New York City for a weekend.
Please (1) _____ me some advice.

Posted at 07.53   Kathryn

Comments

(2) _____ the Metropolitan Museum and
(3) _____ a coffee on the rooftop! There's a fantastic view!

Posted at 09.47   Lindsey

(4) _____ some New York pizza and
(5) _____ an ice cream soda – it's the best in the world!

Posted at 11.15   Emma

(6) _____ to buy a good guidebook. It's easy to get lost.

Posted at 11.41   Dale

(7) _____ in an expensive hotel. They aren't friendly.

Posted at 12.17   Jaime

(8) _____ a good street map. (9) _____
around Manhattan – it's fun!

Posted at 14.43   Duncan

(10) _____ to New York in the winter – it's too cold!

Posted at 15.15   Alan

WHAT'S RIGHT?

(X) Don't to forget your umbrella.

(✓) _____

C   There is one mistake in each sentence. Rewrite the sentences correctly.

1   Don't to visit New York in the winter. _____
2   You go to some shows on Broadway. _____
3   Don't you take a taxi – they're expensive! _____
4   You buying some designer clothes and shoes. _____
5   Don't spending too much money! _____
6   Takes a ride around Central Park. _____

5 VOCABULARY: locations and directions

A Read the directions and mark the route on the map. Then complete the directions with your destination.

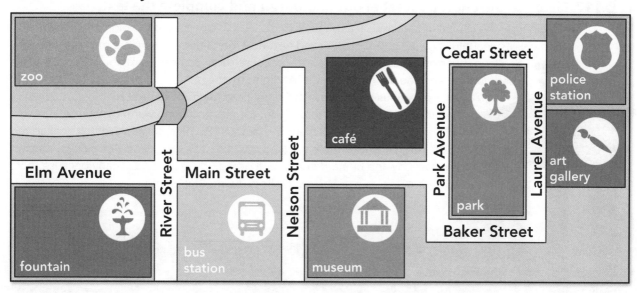

Start at the zoo on River Street. Go over the bridge and straight ahead. Turn left and go straight ahead. Take the second left and go straight ahead. Turn right and go to the end of the street. The _____ is on the corner of Cedar Street and Laurel Avenue, next to the art gallery.

B Look at the map in Exercise A again. Read the directions and write the places.

1 It's on the corner of River Street and Elm Avenue. _____
2 It's opposite the art gallery. _____
3 It's between the museum and the fountain. _____
4 It's next to the police station. _____

C Look at the map in Exercise A again. Write the directions from the zoo to the café.

Start at the zoo on River Street. _____
_____
_____
_____
_____
_____

6 COMMUNICATION STRATEGY: repeating directions to check understanding

A Number the parts of the conversation in the correct order.

☐ A: Ah! First street on the right. OK, thanks.
☐ B: No, the first street on the right.
☐ A: Excuse me, how do I get to the library?
☐ A: Turn left. Then take the first street on the left.
☐ B: First, turn left here and then take the first street on the right.

B 🎧 16 Listen to three conversations. Correct the directions.

1 Go straight ahead and take the third left. _____
2 Take the first left. Then go straight ahead. _____
3 Go straight here and then take the third right. _____

Listen and write

A 🎧 **17 Listen to the short podcast about Edinburgh and complete the text.**

Edinburgh, the capital of Scotland, is a (1) _____ city. Stay in the old part of town, and visit its beautiful (2) _____ and historical monuments. There are many castles in Scotland, but don't miss Edinburgh Castle because there you can learn about Scottish kings and queens, and see the crown jewels. At night, try the (3) _____. This way you can visit famous places from the *Harry Potter* films. It starts at (4) _____ in the cemetery. Don't forget your camera and bring warm clothes. In (5) _____, there is a famous international arts event. It's called the Edinburgh Festival. There are (6) _____, dance, music and theatre shows all day and night. Remember to (7) _____ early because there are over (8) _____ visitors during that month.

B **Read the text and complete these exercises.**

1 Circle the adjectives in the text. Which nouns do they describe?
2 Underline sentences in the text which give reasons. Which words or phrases introduce a reason?

Over to You

C **Choose a place of interest in your town or country. Then make notes about it using these points.**

location _____
adjectives to describe the place _____
accommodation _____
places to visit / reasons for visiting _____
festivals / other information _____
important tips _____

D ✏️ In your notebook, write a paragraph about the place you recommend to tourists. Use your notes in Exercise C and the text in Exercise A to help you. Remember to give reasons for your recommendations, and to use words and expressions to connect your ideas.

> **WRITING TUTOR**
>
> *Don't forget/miss …*
> *Bring …*
> *At night / In August …*
> *There is / There are …*
> *This way / … because …*

DOWN TIME

A Look at these famous places and tourist attractions. Complete the names with the words from the box.

Fountain   Museum   Park   ~~Square~~   Zoo

Red *Square* _____

San Diego _____

Central _____

Guggenheim _____

Trevi _____

B Find the cities for the famous places in Exercise A in the word search and write them. The words can go forwards (→), backwards (←), down (↓) or diagonally (↗).

H	E	R	P	E	T	H	E	B	O
N	R	E	A	A	N	D	I	G	E
E	M	O	R	V	R	L	E	E	R
W	Y	W	H	E	B	I	R	E	N
Y	B	K	Q	A	D	K	S	N	K
O	W	T	O	N	V	Z	L	F	M
R	T	L	A	H	L	F	Q	M	B
K	T	S	T	M	O	S	C	O	W

_____
_____
_____
_____

UNIT 6 DIFFERENT STROKES

1 VOCABULARY: lifestyle adjectives

A 🎧 18 Listen to these words that describe lifestyles. Write the words. Then check the spelling in your Student's Book or a dictionary.

1 _____
2 _____
3 _____
4 _____
5 _____
6 _____

B 🎧 19 Listen to Emily talking about people in her family. Write a word from Exercise A to describe each person's lifestyle.

Mum   Dad

1 _____   2 _____

Karen   Mark   Donna   Emily

3 _____   4 _____   5 _____   6 _____

2 GRAMMAR: present continuous

A Write the –ing form of the verbs from the box in the correct column.

happen   have   ~~live~~   plan   run   study   swim   take   talk   wait   win   write

Add -ing	Drop e and add -ing	Double final consonant and add -ing
	living	

B Look at the picture and complete the sentences with the present continuous form of the verbs from the box.

drink   listen   read   stand   talk

1 Alice _____ a newspaper.
2 Martin and Emma _____ .
3 They _____ coffee.
4 Greg _____ to his MP3 player.
5 Ben _____ next to Alice.

C Write sentences to describe the differences between the pictures. Use the phrases in the box.

> eat ice cream   play with a dog   play the guitar   listen to music
> use a tablet   feed the birds   have a picnic   read a magazine

WHAT'S RIGHT?

(X) The boy is play with a dog.

(✓) _____

1   *In picture 1, the boy is playing with a dog, but in picture 2, he is eating ice cream.*   (*the boy*)

2   _____ (*the girl*)

3   _____ (*the man*)

4   _____ (*the woman*)

5   _____ (*the students*)

3 LISTENING: for numerical information

A 🎧 20 Listen and write the numbers. Listen again and practise saying the sentences.

1   I am _____ years old.
2   The time is _____.
3   My phone number is _____.
4   This building dates from _____.
5   My date of birth is _____ / _____ / _____.

B 🎧 21 Leonardo Oliveira is calling the bank to check his credit card statement. Listen to Leonardo and complete his details.

Name: *Leonardo Oliveira*

Account number: _____

ID number: _____

Amount on statement: £ _____

Problem: There is a charge of £ _____ and he doesn't know what it's for.

Telephone number: _____

4 VOCABULARY: a green lifestyle

A Match the words to make phrases about being green.

1	buy	a)	litter
2	pick up	b)	water
3	reuse	c)	the lights
4	save	d)	a lift
5	get	e)	organic food
6	turn off	f)	bags

B Complete the sentences with words from Exercise A.

HOW TO BE GREEN

1 Don't throw away your plastic bags – _____ them.

2 Don't drive alone in your car – _____ a lift with a friend.

3 Don't waste water – _____ water by fixing leaks.

GLASS   METAL   PAPER   PLASTIC

4 Don't leave litter everywhere – _____ it _____.

5 Don't waste electricity – _____ the lights when you leave a room.

6 Don't use chemicals to grow food – buy _____ food.

5 GRAMMAR: present continuous vs present simple

A Read the conversations. Choose the correct option to complete the sentences.

1. **A:** What do you do / are you doing?
   B: I'm an author. I am writing / write novels.
2. **A:** Where does he go / is he going right now?
   B: He goes / is going home.
3. **A:** What time do they have / are they having lunch every day?
   B: At 1pm usually.
4. **A:** Does she like / Is she liking her new school?
   B: I don't know / am not knowing.

36

B There is one mistake in each pair of sentences. Rewrite the sentences correctly.

WHAT'S RIGHT?

ⓧ I'm loving you.

✓ _____

1 I study now. I have an exam tomorrow.

_____

2 Albert works very hard on his project. He needs to finish it today.

_____

3 Raoul is usually playing squash three times a week. He wants to have a healthy lifestyle.

_____

4 Kirsty isn't knowing Ben. They aren't friends.

_____

C Complete the conversation with the correct form of the verb in brackets.

Sue: Hi, Brad. What (1) _____ you _____ (do) these days?

Brad: I (2) _____ (study) at university at the moment. I (3) _____ (take) classes in computer science this term.

Sue: (4) _____ you _____ (like) your classes?

Brad: Yes, they're fun! I (5) _____ (want) to be a video game designer when I finish. I (6) _____ (play) a lot of video games in my free time. Also, I (7) _____ (work) part-time for a video game company at the moment. I (8) _____ (like) my job a lot!

Sue: That's great. Good luck!

6 WRITING: simple sentences

A Tick (✓) the word that describes the <u>underlined</u> words and phrases in each sentence.

		Subject	Verb	Object
1	Joanna eats <u>organic food</u>.			
2	Ryan <u>recycles</u> bottles and jars.			
3	<u>Martha and Leo</u> waste a lot of water.			
4	I usually ride <u>a bike</u>.			
5	<u>Susanna</u> uses recycled paper.			
6	My sister <u>drives</u> an electric car.			

B Read the sentences. What kind of word is missing: subject, verb or object?

1 *verb* I often _____ to work.
2 _____ We usually recycle our _____.
3 _____ Nowadays people are trying to save _____.
4 _____ Some cars _____ too much petrol.
5 _____ _____ gets a lift to work with her colleague.
6 _____ I always _____ the computer at night.

C Complete the sentences in Exercise B with the words from the box.

energy   my neighbour   newspapers   turn off   use   walk

Read and write

A Read the text about World Environment Day. <u>Underline</u> the green activities.

World Environment Day is an annual event. Every year, countries all around the world organise activities to promote positive environmental action. Maria explains what people are doing in her city in Brazil:

'Today, my friends and I are planting trees in the park, and we're informing people about the ecological problems in the Amazon rainforest. In the city centre, people are cycling or using public transport because today is also a No Car Day. This morning, the local supermarket is only selling local food, and the Green Dream Team is picking up the litter. I always save water, and recycle bottles and paper.'

What are you doing to help?

B Now put a tick (✓) next to the green activities you do.

- ☐ turn off the lights
- ☐ cycle to work/university
- ☐ buy local food
- ☐ get a lift
- ☐ use reusable bags
- ☐ have a shorter shower
- ☐ buy a reusable coffee cup
- ☐ collect rainwater
- ☐ do a cold clothes wash
- ☐ fix water leaks

Over to You

C You are a journalist. You want to write a paragraph about what's happening in your town or city on World Environment Day. But first, plan and organise your ideas!

Think about:
- **Introduction:** What event? Why? Where? When?
- **Development:** What is happening? What do you do to help the environment?
- **Ending:** Short interesting sentence/question to finish.
- What time expressions can you use?

D 🖉 In your notebook, write your paragraph.

WRITING TUTOR

Today, my family is / friends / people in town are …

I usually …

We also …

At the weekend …

Today / At the moment / Now / This morning …

DOWN TIME

A **How green are you? How well informed are you about green issues? Do the quiz to find out. Choose your answers and then check your results.**

1 How do you travel to university or work?
   a) I take public transport.
   b) I cycle or walk.
   c) I drive.
   d) I get a lift to work.

2 Do you reuse bags when you go shopping?
   a) I never reuse bags.
   b) I sometimes reuse bags.
   c) I often reuse bags.
   d) I always reuse bags.

3 How often do you buy organic food?
   a) I never buy organic food.
   b) I sometimes buy organic eggs at the supermarket.
   c) I grow organic vegetables.
   d) I usually buy organic food.

4 Do you leave electrical items on standby when you are not using them?
   a) I sometimes leave items on standby.
   b) I never leave items on standby.
   c) I often leave items on standby.
   d) I always leave items on standby.

5 What do people do on World Environment Day?
   a) take positive environmental action
   b) promote sustainable development
   c) discuss climate change
   d) all of the above

6 How much waste did UK households recycle in 2011/2012?
   a) 13%
   b) 23%
   c) 33%
   d) 43%

7 How much water can people waste if they leave the tap running while they brush their teeth?
   a) around 3 litres
   b) around 7 litres
   c) around 10 litres
   d) around 15 litres

Now check your answers and add up your scores.

	a	b	c	d
1	2	3	0	1
2	0	1	2	3
3	0	1	2	3
4	2	3	1	0
5	1	1	1	3
6	0	1	2	3
7	0	1	2	3

0–6 Your actions are damaging the environment! Find out what you can do to help!

7–13 Not too bad. You are environmentally aware, but you can do more to help the planet!

14+ You are a green star! You know a lot about green issues and you are helping in many ways! Well done!

B **Find the verbs in the word search to complete the phrases. The words can go forwards (→), backwards (←), down (↓) or diagonally (↗).**

1 _____ water
2 _____ the lights
3 _____ bottles and jars
4 _____ paper
5 _____ a lift
6 _____ litter

U	S	E	A	B	R	C
D	E	P	F	G	E	T
G	S	I	N	V	C	U
H	A	C	O	W	Y	R
I	V	K	P	X	C	N
R	E	U	S	E	L	O
J	L	P	Q	Y	E	F
K	M	R	S	T	U	F

UNIT 7 YOU'VE GOT TALENT!

1 VOCABULARY: personality adjectives

A Read the sentences and choose the correct option.

1 George always buys presents for his friends. He's very optimistic / generous / honest.
2 Everyone likes Patricia. She knows a lot of people. She's very clever / patient / friendly.
3 Yumi always makes a list before she goes shopping. She's very organised / generous / optimistic.
4 Steve feels angry when he has to wait for a long time. He's not very reliable / friendly / patient.
5 Fernanda always looks for problems in every situation. She's not very clever / optimistic / honest.
6 Elizabeth is a good friend. Her friends can depend on her for help. She's very patient / reliable / organised.
7 Denise always gets good marks at university. She's very clever / friendly / honest.
8 Stan is always truthful, and you can always believe him. He's very patient / honest / generous.

B Choose one adjective from Exercise A that describes you and one adjective that describes your best friend. Explain why.

I am honest because I always tell the truth.

_____

_____

2 READING: for the main idea

A Look quickly at the text. What kind of text is it?

a) a personality test   b) an advice column   c) a horoscope

LIBRA 23rd September–22nd October

(1) _____ You have no problems making friends this month. Your conversation and humour charm everyone.

(2) _____ Now is not the time to buy a new laptop. Only buy the things you really need.

(3) _____ You're stressed and tired. Drink herbal teas to get more energy.

(4) _____ You have an important decision to make about a colleague. Be honest.

SCORPIO 23rd October–21st November

(5) _____ Be patient with relatives. Don't argue with people close to you.

(6) _____ This month is a good time to start your new diet. Go to the gym, eat fresh fruit and vegetables, cycle to work.

(7) _____ You want to move ahead, but there are many obstacles. Your boss knows that you are reliable, so don't worry.

(8) _____ Don't be too generous this month. You shouldn't spend too much.

B Read the text in Exercise A again. Write the headings in the correct place.

Work (x 2)   Health (x 2)   Family   Money (x 2)   Social life

3 GRAMMAR: *can/can't – ability*

A 🎧 22 **Listen and choose *can* or *can't*.**

1 Elena can / can't play the piano.
2 Peter can / can't dance.
3 I can / can't sing.
4 We can / can't drive.

B 🎧 23 **Listen and tick (✓) the things that Ricky and Bella can do. Cross (✗) the things they can't do.**

	Ricky	Bella
play a sport		
speak another language		
cook		

C **Make sentences about Bella and Ricky. Use *can* and *can't*.**

1 Ricky / play tennis

_____

2 Bella / play a sport

_____

3 Bella and Ricky / speak another language?
   A: _____?
   B: Yes, _____.
4 Bella / cook?
   A: _____?
   B: No, _____.
5 Ricky / cook spaghetti?
   A: _____?
   B: Yes, _____.

WHAT'S RIGHT?

✗ Jeremy can speaks Korean.

✓ _____

D **Put the words in the correct order to form sentences and questions. Sometimes there is more than one correct answer.**

1 Marisa and Julia / speak / can / Italian / .

_____

2 your brother / cook / can / Indian food / ?

_____

3 can / my best friend / sing / and / dance the tango / .

_____

4 I / read music / play the piano / but / I / can / can't / .

_____

5 she / play tennis / swim / can't / but / she / can / .

_____

WHAT'S RIGHT?

✗ They can to play the guitar.

✓ _____

4 VOCABULARY: talents and abilities

A Write the words from the box in the correct column.

> a car   chess   Chinese food   dinner   the guitar
> the piano   to university   to work   traditional dishes

cook	play	drive

B 🎧 24 Listen and write each person's talents below.

1 Chloe can play _____.
  She is good at _____.

2 Alicia is good at _____.
  She likes _____.
  She is good at _____.

3 Tony is good at _____.
  He can speak _____.
  He can cook _____.

5 GRAMMAR: adverbs of manner

A Write the adverbs.

Adjective	Adverb	Adjective	Adverb
slow		good	
easy		bad	
beautiful		fast	
noisy		quiet	

B Rewrite the sentences with *can't* and the adverb form of the adjective in brackets.

1 Sam swims, but he's very slow.
   He can't swim fast. (fast)

2 Victoria speaks Japanese. She's a beginner.
   _____ (fluent)

3 Julia plays chess, but she's not very good.
   _____ (good)

4 Mike talks a lot. He is always very loud.
   _____ (quiet)

5 Robert reads books, but he's slow.
   _____ (quick)

6 My children ride bikes. They're slow riders.
   _____ (fast)

C What can these people do? Write a sentence about each picture. Use *can* and the adverb form of the adjective in brackets.

WHAT'S RIGHT?

Ⓧ She can very well play the piano.

✓ _____

1 Dmitri _____
   _____. (good)

2 Kathy and Sally _____
   _____. (fast)

3 Francesca and Theo _____
   _____. (fluent)

6 COMMUNICATION STRATEGY: showing interest

A Read and choose the best answer.

1 Leona can speak five different languages.
   a) Wow, that's amazing!   b) Ah, that's nice.

2 Frank can cook excellent Thai food.
   a) Yeah? I can cook Indian food.   b) Really? I love Thai food.

3 Sam can play six musical instruments.
   a) That's good.   b) That's incredible!

B 》25 Listen to each conversation. Tick (✓) the conversations in which the first speaker shows interest.

Conversation 1 ☐
Conversation 2 ☐
Conversation 3 ☐

C 》25 Listen again and practise saying the expressions for showing interest with the right intonation.

Listen and write

A 🎧 **26** Listen to each person's profile, and make short notes on their personalities and talents.

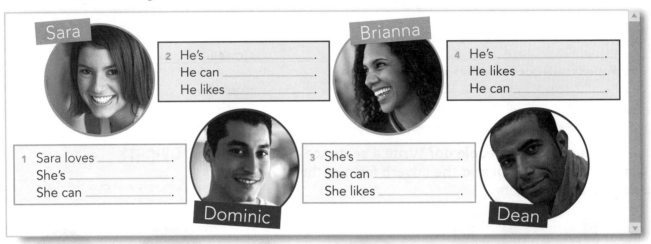

Sara

2 He's _____.
He can _____.
He likes _____.

Brianna

4 He's _____.
He likes _____.
He can _____.

1 Sara loves _____.
She's _____.
She can _____.

Dominic

3 She's _____.
She can _____.
She likes _____.

Dean

B Match the activities to the pictures.

1 do crosswords
2 take salsa classes
3 go to a dinner party
4 go snowboarding
5 visit archaeological sites
6 go to a karaoke evening
7 go to a concert
8 go fishing

C Choose activities in Exercise B for each person in Exercise A. In your notebook, write sentences to say why they like the activities.

Sara likes going to karaoke evenings because she loves music and she can sing.

A

B

C

D

E

F

G

H

Over to You

D Choose three adjectives that describe you. Then, in your notebook, write three things you like and are good at. Give reasons for your examples.

E ✏ Write a profile of yourself. Use your notes in Exercise D and the profiles in Exercise A to help you.

> **WRITING TUTOR**
>
> I'm …
> I can …
> I love …
> I'm good at … / I'm not good at … + gerund

DOWN TIME

A **Play the word game. Follow these instructions.**

- You have five minutes to make as many words as possible from the letters in the grid.
- The letters of the word must be next to each other in the grid.
- Letters can be next to each other horizontally, vertically or diagonally.
- Write your words on the lines.
- Use a dictionary to check any new words.

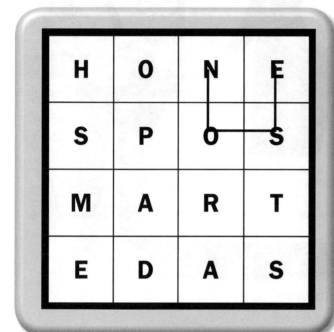

_____
_____
_____
_____
_____
_____
_____
_____
_____
_____
_____

B **Look at these words. Find the missing vowels and write the word.**

    a e i o u

c l v r   _____
f s t   _____
f r n d l y   _____
h n s t   _____
p t n t   _____
r g n s d   _____
p t m s t c   _____
b t f l   _____

C **Complete the crossword.**

Across

2 I can ... French food.
5 I can ... the guitar.
6 Can you ... a car?

Down

1 She is very ... at karate!
3 They can ... Spanish and English.
4 Listen! He can ... opera!

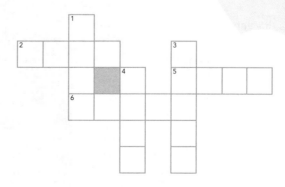

UNIT 8 SHOPPING AROUND

1 VOCABULARY: clothes

A What are Elena and Fabio wearing? Write the words for their clothes.

Elena

_____

_____

_____

Fabio

_____

_____

_____

B Make a list of the clothes you are wearing today.

_____

_____

2 GRAMMAR: this, that, these, those

A Complete the table with this, that, these or those.

	T-shirt	shorts	jeans
Close to the person speaking			
Not close to the person speaking			

B Look at the picture. Complete the conversation. Use this, that, these or those.

Yuko: Oh, I love (1) _____ dress. What a beautiful colour!

Reina: Yes, (2) _____ colour suits you. But what about (3) _____ skirts over there? You should try on (4) _____ long one.

Yuko: Good idea. It's very pretty.

Reina: What about (5) _____ jeans for me? Should I try them on?

Yuko: Yes, and how about one of (6) _____ jumpers, too?

Reina: OK. Where are the changing rooms?

WHAT'S RIGHT?

Ⓧ I like this jeans.

✓ _____

46

3 LISTENING: for numerical information

A))) 27 Listen to the conversations and complete the table.

	Type of clothing	Price
1		£
2		£
3		£
4		£

B))) 28 Look at the photos. How much do you think each item costs? Write your guess below the photo. Then listen to the game show and write the correct answer on the label.

Your guess: _____   Your guess: _____   Your guess: _____

4 VOCABULARY: adjectives for describing gadgets

A))) 29 Listen and write the adjectives. Then check the spelling in your Student's Book or dictionary.

1 _____   3 _____   5 _____
2 _____   4 _____

B))) 30 Listen to the description of each gadget. Choose an adjective from Exercise A that describes it best.

1 _____   2 _____   3 _____   4 _____   5 _____

5 GRAMMAR: comparative adjectives

A Complete the table with the comparative form of each adjective.

Adjective	Comparative form	Adjective	Comparative form
small		popular	*more/less popular*
clever		exciting	
big		bad	
happy		good	
compact		pretty	
up-to-date		expensive	
cheap		easy	
old		slow	
attractive		high	

B Write sentences. Use the comparative form.

1 a games console / ↓ expensive / laptop
   A games console is less expensive than a laptop.

2 an MP3 player / ↑ up-to-date / a CD player
   _____

3 a digital camera / ↑ compact / a film camera
   _____

4 emails / ↑ cheap / phone calls
   _____

5 my old computer / ↑ big / my new computer
   _____

6 desktop computers / ↑ powerful / laptops
   _____

7 my new mobile phone / ↓ user-friendly / my old one
   _____

8 my new office chair / ↓ comfortable / my old chair
   _____

9 this e-reader / ↑ easy to use / that e-reader
   _____

10 his desk / ↑ small / yours
   _____

WHAT'S RIGHT?

(X) This computer is more better than that one.

(✓) _____

C There is one mistake in each sentence. Rewrite the sentences correctly.

1 An electronic dictionary is good than a book dictionary.
   _____

2 Our new TV is more larger than our old TV.
   _____

3 This camera is smaller my mobile phone.
   _____

4 Phone calls on the internet are more cheap than by mobile phone.
   _____

5 News on the internet is up-to-date than the newspaper.
   _____

6 My old computer bigger than my new one.
   _____

7 My new tablet is user-friendly than my old one.
   _____

8 My laptop is more heavy than yours.

48

D Look at the pictures. Use adjectives from Exercise A to write correct sentences.

1 _____

2 _____

3 _____

6 WRITING: compound sentences

A Choose the best option to complete the sentences.

1 These shoes are really small, and / but / or they aren't comfortable.
2 I want to buy a new laptop, and / but / or they're very expensive.
3 Do you want to buy this T-shirt now and / but / or do you want to try it on first?
4 I like sending emails, and / but / or I prefer talking on the phone.
5 You can buy a computer here and / but / or you can get one online.
6 This new MP3 player is more compact, and / but / or it isn't heavy.

B Choose the best ending to complete the sentences.

1 This new laptop is very versatile, and …
　a) it is powerful.
　b) it is too complicated.

2 My new computer is not compact, but …
　a) it is expensive.
　b) it is user-friendly.

3 You can call me or …
　a) you can use the phone.
　b) you can send me an email.

4 I like to buy clothes online, but …
　a) I sometimes get the wrong size.
　b) I sometimes save money.

Read and write

A Read an advert and user ratings on a website about a new smartphone, and answer the questions.

HOME   PRODUCTS   REVIEWS   BUY   SEARCH

Are you looking for this year's best smartphone? Buy the R2 Sonic! It's very user-friendly and has a larger memory than the previous model. The bigger screen is good for photos. Choose black or blue headphones. It has everything you need for a great price!

R2 Sonic
★★★☆☆

KAREN ★★☆☆☆
The R2 Sonic comes with blue headphones. They're cool but heavy! There are lots of games, but they aren't up-to-date games.

PETER ★☆☆☆☆
I don't know about this phone. It holds 3,000 more songs than the last model, but I don't need 12,000 songs, and it's more expensive.

DIETER ★★★★☆
I love this phone. It's more compact than the previous model, but it has a bigger screen. It can store more photos and songs, and the internet is faster because the memory is more powerful. I'd definitely recommend it!

1   Does Karen like the phone? Why or why not? _____
2   Why doesn't Peter like the phone? _____
3   What does Dieter like about the phone? _____

Over to You

B Choose a product to write a recommendation for. Write what you like and don't like about it.

Product: _____

Things I like: _____

Things I don't like: _____

C ✎ In your notebook, write a product recommendation to post on a website. Use the advert in Exercise A and your ideas from Exercise B to help you. Remember to use *and*, *but* and *or* to connect your ideas and write longer sentences.

WRITING TUTOR

It is … and …
I like …, but …
I don't like … because …
I don't know about …
It comes with …
You can choose a … or a …
I'd definitely recommend it!

DOWN TIME

A Find the 15 clothes items in the word search and write them below.
The words can go forwards (→), down (↓) or diagonally (↗).

O	P	E	B	O	S	H	O	T	P	P	R	J
T	R	A	I	N	E	R	S	T	U	M	I	A
K	S	W	E	J	U	M	P	E	R	T	I	E
H	U	H	O	T	K	S	E	R	N	I	J	C
A	I	L	I	D	R	E	S	S	E	S	A	C
N	T	K	H	R	P	A	T	H	J	H	C	P
D	S	B	O	O	T	S	S	W	O	I	K	U
B	H	N	E	A	T	H	N	O	E	R	E	R
A	S	K	I	R	T	O	O	P	A	T	T	S
G	W	D	V	U	J	E	A	N	S	U	I	S
K	T	T	R	O	U	S	E	R	S	R	T	H

_____ _____ _____ _____ _____
_____ _____ _____ _____ _____
_____ _____ _____ _____ _____

B Link the word parts to make a complete word.
Then match them to their description.

che	up	erful	frie
tive	pact		attrac
user-	pow	date	expen
sive	atile	-to-	
ndly	vers	ap	com

1 not expensive _____
2 small _____
3 stores a lot of information _____
4 easy to use _____
5 looks nice _____
6 can do different things _____
7 costs a lot of money _____
8 modern _____

UNIT 9 LET'S EAT

1 VOCABULARY: food

A Label the pictures with the words from the box.

> bananas bread broccoli cheese
> chicken meat milk oranges peas
> potatoes rice yoghurt watermelon

1 _____ 2 _____ 3 _____

4 _____ 5 _____ 6 _____ 7 _____ 8 _____

9 _____ 10 _____ 11 _____ 12 _____ 13 _____

B Put the words from Exercise A in the correct column.

Fruit	Vegetables	Carbohydrates	Protein	Dairy products

C Answer these questions about the food in Exercise A.

1 Which of these foods do you eat every day? _____
2 Which foods do you rarely eat? _____

2 GRAMMAR: countable and uncountable nouns with *some, any, much, many*

A Complete the table with the words from the box.

> apple banana biscuits bread butter crisps
> meat milk onions potatoes tomato watermelon

Countable nouns (singular)	Countable nouns (plural)	Uncountable nouns

B Complete the sentences. Use *a, an, much, many, some* or *any*.

1 I'm really hungry. I want _____ big sandwich and _____ juice.
2 I want _____ coffee, please. I don't want _____ milk – just a little.
3 Are you hungry? There aren't _____ biscuits left – only two or three, but I think there is _____ bread.
4 There isn't _____ rice. Let's cook _____ pasta.

C There is one mistake in each sentence. Rewrite the sentences correctly.

1 I don't want an cream with my pie. _____
2 I don't want some vegetables. _____
3 I want any rice with my fish. _____
4 How much bananas do we have? _____
5 Do you have a bread? _____
6 Do you want biscuit? _____

3 COMMUNICATION STRATEGY: using phone language

A Number the parts of the conversation in the correct order. Then choose the correct option.

☐ It's Alice, and my number is 01568 398431. Thanks!
☐ Hi. Is Janice there?
☐ I'm sorry. She's out. Can I take a message?
☐ No problem.
☐ Yes, please. Can you ask her to call me tonight? It's important.
☐ Sure. What's your name?

The conversation is formal / informal.

B 》31 Complete the conversation with the phrases from the box. Then listen and check your answers.

| could I | could you | isn't here | thank you | would you |

A: Good afternoon. **(1)** _____ speak to Mr Brown, please?
B: I'm sorry. He **(2)** _____ at the moment.
    (3) _____ like to leave a message?
A: Yes, please. **(4)** _____ ask him to call me back?
    My name's Mike Thompson, and my number is 01460 013192.
B: Yes, of course.
A: **(5)** _____ .
B: You're welcome.

While you were out

Message for:	Helen Stevens
Message taken by:	Lily
Caller:	Fred Stevens
Message:	Call him back on 01450 323195.

C Write a conversation like the one in Exercise B. Use the information in the phone message.

Fred: *Good afternoon.* _____
Lily: _____
       _____
Fred: _____
       _____
Lily: _____
Fred: _____
Lily: _____

4 GRAMMAR: verb phrases

A Complete the conversation. Use the infinitive or base form of the verbs from the box.

come	get	have	make	order	stay	take	try

A: Would you like (1) _____ over to my house for dinner tonight?

B: I'd love (2) _____ dinner with you but I need (3) _____ at home and finish my essay tonight. How about tomorrow night?

A: Great! Do you want (4) _____ Chinese food? We could (5) _____ a takeaway.

B: A takeaway sounds good. Let's (6) _____ that new Chinese restaurant.

A: OK. How about 7pm?

B: Let's (7) _____ it 7.30, OK? I have (8) _____ some books back to the library first.

A: Sure! See you tomorrow.

B Match to make complete sentences.

1 Would you …   a) to book a table for lunch, only for dinner.
2 Do you …   b) to buy some tomatoes for the soup.
3 Let's …   c) go for pizza on Saturday.
4 You don't have …   d) like to go out for lunch tomorrow?
5 I need …   e) want to eat Indian food tonight?

5 VOCABULARY: ordering in a restaurant

A Match to complete the phrases.

1 green   a) chicken
2 grilled   b) salad
3 roast   c) soup
4 vegetable   d) fish

B Label the pictures with a phrase from Exercise A.

1 _____

2 _____

3 _____

4 _____

C Look at the menu. Write the words from the box in the correct place.

Starters   Beverages   Desserts   Main courses

MENU

1 _____

Soup of the day	£3.95
Green salad	£2.95
Stuffed mushrooms	£4.95

2 _____

Roast chicken with vegetables	£10.95
Grilled fish with potatoes	£9.95
Spaghetti and meatballs	£7.50

3 _____

Apple tart	£3.99
Cake	£3.99
Fruit salad	£2.99

4 _____

Still/sparkling water	£1.00
Juice, soft drink	£1.99
Coffee, tea	£1.50

D »🎧 **32** Now listen to Lucy and Dan ordering from the menu. On the menu, circle what Dan wants to eat. Underline what Lucy wants to eat.

E How much does Lucy need to pay and how much does Dan need to pay? What is the total cost of their order?

Lucy's order: _____
Dan's order: _____
Total: _____

6 READING: scanning for specific information

A Choose the best menu for each person.

1 ☐ Daniela loves fish. She doesn't like cakes. She prefers fruit.
2 ☐ Susanna is a vegetarian, and she loves ice cream.
3 ☐ Michael is on a diet. He doesn't want to eat fried food or carbohydrates.
4 ☐ Bill doesn't like red meat, but he eats chicken and fish. He loves cake.

MENU 1

STARTER:
Onion soup

❋

MAIN COURSE:
Spaghetti with cheese sauce

❋

DESSERT:
Apple tart and ice cream

MENU 2

STARTER:
Tomato salad

❋

MAIN COURSE:
Roast chicken with green salad

❋

DESSERT:
Strawberries

MENU 3

STARTER:
Stuffed mushrooms

❋

MAIN COURSE:
Fried fish with rice

❋

DESSERT:
Fruit salad and ice cream

MENU 4

STARTER:
Broccoli soup

❋

MAIN COURSE:
Chicken and potato salad

❋

DESSERT:
Cake

B Which menu in Exercise A is your favourite? Why?

My favourite menu is Menu ... because ...

Listen and write

A 🎧 33 Listen to the radio show. Circle the ingredients you need to make the recipe.

spinach
bread
strawberries
nuts
broccoli
potatoes
cream

butter
oil
melon
vinegar
salt
paprika
onion

B 🎧 33 Listen again and number the instructions in the correct order.

☐ Cook these for about one minute.

☐ Add the nuts.

☐ Pour this over the salad.

☐ Combine the oil, vinegar, paprika and onion.

☐ Put the spinach, strawberries and nuts in a bowl.

☐ Melt the butter over a medium heat.

Over to You

C ✏️ Choose a salad you like and know how to prepare. In your notebook, write the recipe, giving the list of ingredients and the instructions.

DOWN TIME

A Read the clues and complete the crossword.

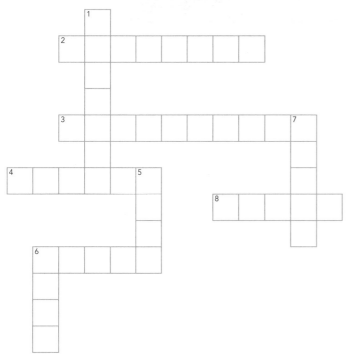

Across
2 Cheese and milk are dairy …
3 You should eat five portions of fruit and … each day.
4 Soft … often contain a lot of sugar.
6 Apples, pears and bananas are types of …
8 Ice … is very good to eat in the summer.

Down
1 Meat and beans are … They give you energy.
5 Too much … is bad for your health.
6 … is caught in the sea.
7 Green … is a popular starter.

B Read the ingredients for the dish and guess what the recipe is for. Write the name of the dish.

Recipe for: _____

For the pastry:
250 g flour
½ teaspoon salt
140 g butter
6 tablespoons cold water

For the filling:
5 apples (cut into small pieces)
1 large lemon, juiced
100 g dark brown sugar
1½ tablespoons flour
¼ teaspoon cinnamon
2 teaspoons milk

1 GRAMMAR: past simple – affirmative statements

A Complete the table with the past simple form of the verbs from the box.

> carry decide explain like live marry
> play prepare stay study try watch

Regular past simple verbs

Add -ed	Add -d	Change *y* to *i* and add -ed

B Complete the table.

Irregular past simple verbs

Base form	Past simple form	Base form	Past simple form
do		meet	
know			spoke
	went		was/were
give		read	
	got		told

C Complete the paragraph with the past simple form of the verbs from the box.

> be eat give go have meet see take

WHAT'S RIGHT?

ⓧ I writed you a postcard last week.

✓ _____

Looking for holiday ideas?

Share experiences and get ideas for fun holidays here!

We (1) _____ to the Sundance Film Festival on our last holiday. It (2) _____ a fantastic experience. We (3) _____ a lot of cool films and we (4) _____ some famous actors. (They (5) _____ us their autographs!) We (6) _____ a lot of photos of film stars. And we (7) _____ in some fabulous restaurants. We (8) _____ a wonderful time and we recommend this film festival for all film fans!

SUBMIT COMMENT

2 VOCABULARY: adjectives with -ed and -ing

A Choose the correct option to complete the sentences.

1   It's my birthday party tomorrow. I'm really exciting / excited about it.
2   We watched a terrible film on TV last night. It was very boring / bored.
3   Tanya worked on this homework all night, and today she's just so tiring / tired.
4   I'm reading a great book right now. It's amazing / amazed.
5   I love playing basketball, but my friends aren't interesting / interested in sport.

B Complete the two sentences for each picture. Use an adjective from Exercise A with -ed or -ing.

Marta

Francisco

Diana

1   Marta's job is _____.
    By the end of the day she's
    really _____.

2   The football match is very
    _____. Francisco
    is _____ about
    the football match.

3   Diana's new boyfriend is really
    _____. She
    listened to him for an hour and
    she was so _____.

3 GRAMMAR: past simple – questions and negative statements

A Complete the questions and answers about Cathy's and Bill's weekend. Use the information in the table.

	Cathy	Bill
ate out	✓	✗
cooked dinner at home	✗	✓
met friends	✓	✓
watched TV	✗	✗

1   A: _____ Cathy
        _____ out?
    B: Yes, _____.

2   A: _____ Bill
        _____ out?
    B: No, _____.

3   A: _____ Cathy and Bill
        _____ friends?
    B: Yes, _____.

4   A: _____ Cathy and Bill
        _____ TV?
    B: No, _____.

5   A: What _____ Cathy
        _____ at the weekend?
    B: She _____ dinner
        at home. She ate out and met friends.

6   A: What _____ Bill
        _____ at the weekend?
    B: He _____ out. He
        cooked dinner at home and met friends.

B 🔊 34 **Complete the questions. Then listen and check your answers.**

1 _____ did you do on Friday night?
2 _____ did you go?
3 _____ you have a good time?
4 _____ did you go with?
5 _____ was the food?
6 _____ it very expensive?

C 🔊 34 **Match the answers to the questions in Exercise B. Listen again to check.**

a) ☐ Oh, fantastic. I love Thai food.
b) ☐ Yes, it was great.
c) ☐ I went out for dinner.
d) ☐ With my girlfriend.
e) ☐ Not too bad, actually.
f) ☐ To the new Thai restaurant. It's fantastic.

4 LISTENING: understanding the main idea

A 🔊 35 **Listen to these conversations. Choose the main topic of each one.**

1 a) an exam   b) a holiday   c) an accident
2 a) a business meeting   b) an exam   c) a holiday
3 a) a holiday   b) a football match   c) a celebration

B 🔊 35 **Listen again. Is each conversation about a positive or a negative experience? Choose the correct option.**

1 positive / negative
2 positive / negative
3 positive / negative

C 🔊 35 **Listen again and write any key words that helped you identify the main idea in each conversation.**

1 _____
2 _____
3 _____

5 WRITING: sequencing and connecting ideas

A Number the pictures in the correct order to make a story about Frank.

B Write Frank's story. Use connecting words: *first, then, after that, finally.*

Yesterday morning, Frank was on his way to meet some friends
when he found ...

_____

_____

_____

_____

_____

_____

6 VOCABULARY: memorable experiences

A Complete the sentences with the past simple form of the verbs from the box.

get (x 2)   see (x 2)   take (x 2)

1 Martine _____ a famous person at the airport.
2 Frank _____ a photo of Alicia Keys at a concert.
3 Emma _____ a fantastic gift from her parents – a new camera!
4 We _____ an amazing concert last weekend.
5 Rick _____ a special letter from his favourite film star.
6 Miranda _____ a trip to Amsterdam for her birthday.

B Match the sentences to make conversations.

1 I saw an amazing concert last night.
2 I got a special letter in the post yesterday.
3 I saw a famous film star in the shopping centre.
4 I got a birthday present from my boyfriend.
5 I saw a film about whales on TV last night.
6 I took some photos of all my classmates.

a) Wow! Who was it?
b) That sounds good. Was it interesting?
c) Oh, yes? Can I see them?
d) That sounds exciting. Who was it from?
e) Really? Who was the band?
f) Oh, yeah? What did you get?

Read and write

A Read this blog entry about Maria's experience. Look at the underlined words in the text. Match them to their function.

I can't believe it! Last night I went out with some friends. We were in a restaurant when suddenly I saw the most gorgeous man ♥!

It felt like I knew him, <u>but</u> I wasn't sure at first. Then, suddenly, I realised – of course I knew him! He is the singer of my favourite band. I love their music <u>and</u> I love him, too! I was really excited and nervous …

My friends told me to go and say hi, <u>so</u> I got up and walked to his table. <u>Then</u>, when I got there, I was so nervous that I hit the table and spilt his drink. I was really embarrassed, but he was very nice and didn't mind. <u>After that</u>, I asked him for his autograph.

He was so amazing. Now I love him more than ever! ☺

Maria

Contrast: _____   Consequence: _____
Addition: _____   Sequence: _____ _____

B Now read the text again and put the events in chronological order.

Maria felt anxious.	_____	Maria's friends said something to her.	_____
Maria went out with friends.	_____	The man gave something to Maria.	_____
Maria recognised the man.	_____	Maria had a small accident.	_____

C Complete the questions that Maria's friend Annie asks about her experience. Then write Maria's answers.

Annie: Where (1) _____ you go?
Maria: (2) _____
Annie: (3) _____ did you go with?
Maria: (4) _____
Annie: (5) _____ happened?
Maria: (6) _____
_____
Annie: (7) _____ did you feel?
Maria: (8) _____

Over to You

D Now think about a memorable event that happened to you. Use key words only to answer Annie's questions in Exercise C about your memory.

1 _____
2 _____
3 _____
4 _____

E ✏ Now use the blog entry in Exercise A and your notes in Exercise D to help you write about your memorable event. Remember to use linking words to connect and organise your text.

> **WRITING TUTOR**
>
> I was …
> I went …
> It felt …
> Then / After that, …
> I jumped when the phone rang.
> Suddenly …
> Now, …

DOWN TIME

A Complete the crossword with the past simple form of these verbs. Time yourself!

1 see
2 watch
3 like
4 be
5 carry
6 listen
7 put
8 eat
9 find
10 practise
11 meet
12 try
13 return

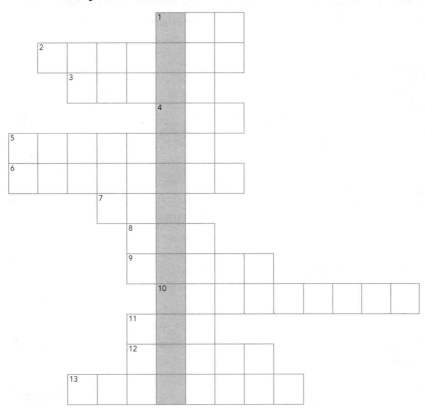

B Where did the girl go? The letters in the shaded boxes spell the words for the answer.

C Choose the phrases that are INCORRECT.

1 a) an amazing hotel   b) an amazed hotel   c) a boring hotel
2 a) a tiring journey   b) a tired man   c) an interested book
3 a) do a party   b) do exercise   c) do sport
4 a) see a concert   b) see a picture   c) see a trip
5 a) take a photo   b) make a photo   c) take a tour
6 a) I'm tiring after the trip.   b) I'm tired after the trip.   c) I'm excited after the trip.

D Put these words in alphabetical order. Time yourself!

bored	interested	anything	concert	night
interesting	boring	show	who	nothing
birthday	exciting	when	cheese	yoghurt
amazed	what	famous	trip	music
shopping	fantastic	weekend	amazing	chicken

UNIT 11 GREAT LIVES

1 READING: scanning for specific information

A Scan the descriptions to find the answers to the questions below. The answer may be more than one person.

Aung San Suu Kyi is the leader of the democratic party in Burma. She won the Nobel Peace Prize in 1991. She became a member of the Burmese Parliament in 2012 after many years under house arrest. She fights every day for the rights of Burmese people.

Chico Mendes was an environmentalist who fought against deforestation in Brazil. He died in 1988 trying to save the Amazon from destruction.

Marco Polo was a Venetian explorer who was born around 1254. He explored distant countries like India and China. He learnt many languages and wrote descriptions of everything he saw.

Jane Goodall was born in England in 1934. She is a naturalist who studied the life patterns of chimpanzees. She works in Tanzania to protect the chimpanzees and to educate children about her work.

Juliana Rotich was born and grew up in Kenya, and later studied IT in the USA. She started a website called *Ushahidi* (meaning 'testimony' in Swahili) to report violence around the world. She also fights to protect forests in Africa.

Stephen Hawking is a British scientist and author. Despite suffering from the debilitating illness Amyotrophic Lateral Sclerosis (ALS), his work in physics and cosmology is groundbreaking, and he wrote the best-selling book, *A Brief History of Time*.

1 Who tries/tried to save trees?

_____ and _____

2 Who was born in the 13th century?

_____

3 Who tries to save animals?

_____

4 Who fights for democracy?

_____

5 Who is a famous scientist?

_____

6 Who won a prize?

_____

B Imagine you meet one of these people. Write two questions to ask him/her.

_____

_____

2 GRAMMAR: past simple with *when* clauses

A Put the words in the correct order to form sentences with *when*.

1 When / had / Sam / got home, / a shower / he /

   _____

2 Danuta / speak English / she / learnt to / when / was / four

   _____

3 the Opera House / they / saw / Mike and Patty / when / visited / Sydney

   _____

4 she / Emi / was 16, / to the USA / When / went

   _____

5 working / started / he / when / was 21 / Steve

   _____

6 were 18 / Alannah and Kate / they / went / backpacking / when

   _____

B Rewrite each pair of sentences to form one sentence, using a *when* clause. Use the correct punctuation.

1 I saw the crocodile. I screamed.

   _____

2 Rosa got her first bicycle. She was 12 years old.

   _____

3 We went to India. We visited the Taj Mahal.

   _____

4 Gustav graduated from university. His parents gave him a ticket for a trip around the world.

   _____

5 Sarah learnt to speak Portuguese. She lived in Brazil.

   _____

3 VOCABULARY: life events

A »⌕36 Listen to a description of the life of the writer Isabel Allende. Number the events in the correct order.

- ☐ She had her daughter Paula.
- ☐ She had her son Nicolás.
- ☐ She became a US citizen.
- ☐ She got married.
- ☐ She moved to Venezuela.
- ☐ She published her first novel.
- ☐ She left school.
- ☐ She was born in Lima, Peru.

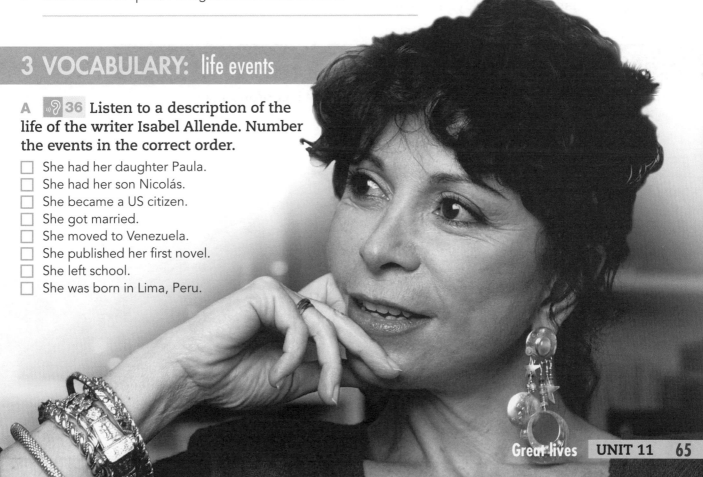

B ⟩》36 **Complete the questions about Isabel Allende. Then listen again and match them to the answers.**

1	*When did she leave school?* (When / leave school)	a)	In 1962.
2	_____ (When / get married)	b)	In 2003.
3	_____ (When / become a US citizen)	c)	In 1982.
4	_____ (When / have her second child)	d)	In 1963.
5	_____ (Where / grow up)	e)	In 1966.
6	_____ (When / born)	f)	In 1942.
7	_____ (Where / born)	g)	In 1958.
8	_____ (When / move to Venezuela)	h)	In 1975.
9	_____ (When / have her first child)	i)	In Chile.
10	_____ (When / publish her first novel)	j)	In Lima, Peru.

4 COMMUNICATION STRATEGY: taking time to think

A Complete the conversation with the phrases from the box.

> I can't remember   I'm not sure, but
> Just a second   Let me think   Oh, yeah   Well

Vicky: Mike, do you want to try this literary quiz?

Mike: (1) _____, I'm not good at literature, but why not … go ahead.

Vicky: OK, question one. Who wrote *The Merchant of Venice*?

Mike: (2) _____. That's easy – Shakespeare!

Vicky: Yes, that's right. And who wrote *The Old Man and the Sea*?

Mike: (3) _____. Um, was it Hemingway?

Vicky: Correct! And how many books are there in the *Harry Potter* series?

Mike: Um, (4) _____ … I think there are six.

Vicky: No, seven! And what's the name of the main character in *Twilight*?

Mike: (5) _____, um, hmm, (6) _____.

Vicky: It's Bella.

B ⟩》37 **Listen and check your answers.**

5 GRAMMAR: direct and indirect objects

A Complete the conversations with the correct object pronouns.

1 A: Did you invite Sally to your party?
   B: No, I don't know _____ very well.

2 A: Is that a new jacket?
   B: Yes, I bought _____ in the sale last week.

3 A: When are Tony and Sue coming?
   B: I'm not sure. Let's call _____.

4 A: What are your plans for the weekend?
   B: We don't know yet. Ask _____ tomorrow!

5 A: Where did Bill and Angie go on holiday?
   B: I don't know. They didn't tell _____.

6 A: Is Pete back from his holiday?
   B: Yes, I saw _____ in class yesterday.

B Rewrite each sentence with direct and indirect object pronouns.

1 My mum bought the jacket for me for my birthday.
She _____ .

2 They gave my father the watch when he retired.
They _____ .

3 I sent an email to my sister this morning.
I _____ .

4 We showed our friends the new house last week.
We _____ .

5 My brother gave the book to me when I graduated.
He _____ .

6 My husband bought some flowers for me on our anniversary.
He _____ .

6 VOCABULARY: historical events

A Write the past simple form of the verbs in the table.

Base form	Past simple form	Base form	Past simple form
build		explore	
win		fight	
compose		invent	
discover		write	

B Complete the questions with one of the past simple verbs from Exercise A. Use each verb once only.

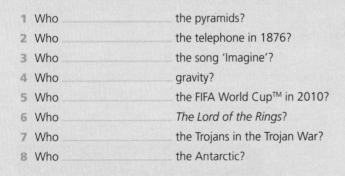

Test your general knowledge

1 Who _____ the pyramids?

2 Who _____ the telephone in 1876?

3 Who _____ the song 'Imagine'?

4 Who _____ gravity?

5 Who _____ the FIFA World Cup™ in 2010?

6 Who _____ *The Lord of the Rings*?

7 Who _____ the Trojans in the Trojan War?

8 Who _____ the Antarctic?

C Match the questions from Exercise B to these answers.

a ☐ Spain
b ☐ Ernest Shackleton
c ☐ Isaac Newton
d ☐ J.R.R. Tolkien
e ☐ John Lennon
f ☐ the Ancient Egyptians
g ☐ the Achaeans
h ☐ Alexander Graham Bell

Listen and write

A 🎧 38 **Listen to a film critic and answer the questions.**

1 Does the film critic recommend the film?

_____

2 What film genre is it?

_____

3 What didn't women usually do at that time?

_____

B 🎧 38 **Listen again and complete the sentences.**

a The film is called *Becoming Jane,* and it's about the life of the _____ Jane Austen.

b Jane Austen was born in _____.

c The story in the film starts when Jane started _____.

d Her family wanted Jane _____.

e But Jane _____ with a poor lawyer.

f It's a romantic and _____ film.

C **Match the sentences in Exercise B to these headings. Then put the headings in the correct order.**

☐ Main character   _____
☐ Change in storyline   _____
☐ Writer's opinion of film   _____
☐ Development of storyline   _____
☐ Introduction to story   _____
☐ Title and main idea of story   _____

Over to You

D **Decide if the film adjectives in the box are positive or negative, and write them in the table.**

boring enjoyable exciting fascinating fast moving funny
happy imaginative predictable scary slow unpredictable

Positive	Negative

E **Think of a film or book you want to recommend to a friend. Make some notes about it using the headings in Exercise C. Use key words only.**

F ✏️ **In your notebook, write your recommendation. Use the headings in Exercise C and your notes in Exercise E to help you. Think about the structure and vocabulary.**

WRITING TUTOR

I read/saw … when …
It was …
The main characters were …
I liked / didn't like …
This was a time when …
The story begins when …
The film is about …

DOWN TIME

A Rearrange the letters in the circles to make words from the unit.

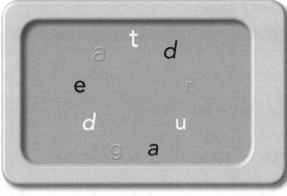

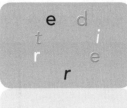

_ _ _ _ _ _ _

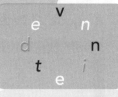

_ _ _ _ _ _ _ _

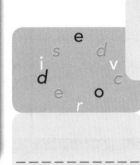

_ _ _ _ _ _ _ _

_ _ _ _ _ _ _ _ _

_ _ _ _ _

B Solve the brain teasers.

1 A family took a trip.
– Mum sat behind her daughter.
– Dad sat next to Mum.
– The brother read a newspaper.

Who drove the car?

_____

2 There are 40 students in your class, but only a quarter of them came to class on time. Later on, 15 students came, but a third of those 15 left to go to lunch.

How many students remained?

_____

3 Cruise Line cruises has 3,500 places available. Different travel companies made 1,270 reservations in total on the first day. A group of graduates reserved 640 spaces on the second day, and two other agencies reserved 370 spaces each.

How many spaces are left for the cruise?

_____

UNIT 12 IN THE NEAR FUTURE

1 GRAMMAR: present continuous as future

A Look at Pete's plans for the week. Choose T (true) or F (false).

Monday	Friday
	9pm Dancing with Daniela
Tuesday	Saturday
7pm Go to the cinema with Anna	10.30am Football with Andy and Jim
	7pm Meet Jerry and Amy for dinner
Wednesday	Sunday
	1pm Lunch with my sister
Thursday	NOTES
1pm Meet Liz for lunch at Brown's café	

1 Pete and Liz are going dancing on Friday.   T / F
2 Pete is having lunch with his sister on Sunday.   T / F
3 Pete is going to the cinema on Monday.   T / F
4 Pete is playing football with Andy and Jim on Saturday morning. T / F

B Look at Pete's diary again. Complete the sentences using the present continuous.

1 A: What _____ on Tuesday night?
   B: He's going to the cinema.
2 A: Who _____ to the cinema with?
   B: With Anna.
3 A: Where _____ Liz for lunch?
   B: At Brown's café.
4 A: What time _____ Jerry and Amy on Saturday?
   B: At 7pm.
5 A: _____ football on Saturday morning?
   B: Yes, he is.
6 A: _____ anything on Monday night?
   B: No, he isn't.

> ### WHAT'S RIGHT?
> ✗ Do you go to the cinema tomorrow night?
> ✓ _____

C There is one mistake in each sentence. Rewrite the sentences correctly.

1 What you are doing tomorrow night? _____
2 They watching a football match on Saturday. _____
3 Are your friend staying at home this weekend? _____
4 They eat out in a Chinese restaurant tonight. _____
5 I am study for an exam tonight. _____
6 They not are working here next week. _____
7 We are visit my parents tonight. _____

2 LISTENING: understanding the main idea

A 🔊 **39** Listen and decide which photo matches the main idea of the conversation. Choose the correct number.

1  2

B 🔊 **39** Listen again and write down any key words that are repeated.

_____

_____

C 🔊 **39** Answer these questions. Then listen again and check your answers.

1 Where is Jim going for his holiday?

_____

2 What is Jim planning to do on his holiday?

_____

3 What is his ideal holiday?

_____

4 What does his friend think about his holiday?

_____

3 VOCABULARY: phrases with *go*

A Label the pictures with the words from the box.

| dancing   horse riding   running |

1 _____ 2 _____ 3 _____

B 🔊 **40** Listen to the conversations. Write sentences with *go* to describe the people's activities.

1 *They are* _____

2 _____

3 _____

4 _____

4 GRAMMAR: *going to*

A Complete the sentences with *going to* and the verbs in brackets.

1 I am planning to go to Italy. I _____ (*improve*) my Italian.
2 Tito wants to buy a car. But first he _____ (*learn*) how to drive.
3 Tomorrow is Uma's birthday. Her sister _____ (*bake*) a cake for her.
4 We don't have any money. We _____ (*not do*) anything this weekend.
5 Gino and Sam have an exam tomorrow. They _____ (*not go out*) tonight.

B Complete the questions with *going to* and the verbs in brackets. Then complete the short answers.

1 A: Where _____ (*go*)?
  B: To Italy.
2 A: What _____ (*do*) there?
  B: Visit art galleries and learn about art.
3 A: Who _____ (*go*) with?
  B: With my girlfriend.
4 A: How long _____ (*stay*) there?
  B: For two months.
5 A: _____ (*study*) Italian?
  B: Yes, I _____.
6 A: _____ (*study*) Italian, too?
  B: No, she _____. She's going to study fashion design.

C Read the descriptions and write what these people are going to do. Use the words from the box.

| be a lawyer | get up earlier | go running | go to China |
| read magazines in English | save money | study harder |

1 Mary is studying law at university.
  She *is going to be a lawyer*.
2 Frank doesn't have enough money to buy a car.
  He _____.
3 I want to learn Chinese.
  I _____.
4 Elizabeth's marks are not good.
  She _____.
5 Frank and Julia are always late for work.
  They _____.
6 We want to exercise more.
  We _____.
7 They want to learn English.
  They _____.

WHAT'S RIGHT?

(✗) They going to go out tonight.

(✓) _____

5 VOCABULARY: intentions

A 🔊 41 Listen to Toshi and Pete talking about what they are going to start and stop doing. Complete the table.

	Toshi	Pete
start		
stop		

B Complete the sentences about Toshi and Pete.

1 Toshi is going to start _____ and _____ .
2 Pete is going to stop _____ and _____ .
3 Toshi and Pete are both going to start _____ .

6 WRITING: sequencing and connecting ideas

A Sergio wants to be a film director like the man in the picture. Number the steps in the best order.

☐ buy a video camera
☐ start saving money
☐ enter a film competition
☐ stop spending money on clothes and CDs
☐ take a course in film directing
☐ write a film script
☐ make a short film

B Write the steps using sequencing words like *first*, *then*, *next*, *after that* and *finally* to connect your ideas.

Sergio wants to be a film director. This is his plan. First, he's going to

_____
_____
_____
_____
_____

C Read the text that you wrote in Exercise B. Check your spelling and punctuation carefully.

Read and write

A Read the website and tick (✓) the activities you want to do in the future.

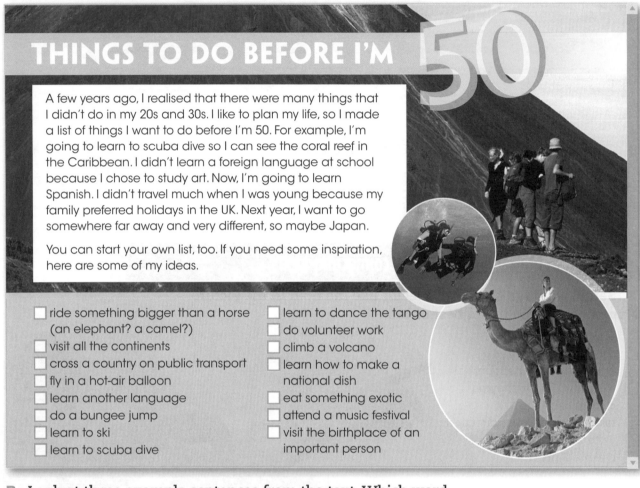

THINGS TO DO BEFORE I'M 50

A few years ago, I realised that there were many things that I didn't do in my 20s and 30s. I like to plan my life, so I made a list of things I want to do before I'm 50. For example, I'm going to learn to scuba dive so I can see the coral reef in the Caribbean. I didn't learn a foreign language at school because I chose to study art. Now, I'm going to learn Spanish. I didn't travel much when I was young because my family preferred holidays in the UK. Next year, I want to go somewhere far away and very different, so maybe Japan.

You can start your own list, too. If you need some inspiration, here are some of my ideas.

- ☐ ride something bigger than a horse (an elephant? a camel?)
- ☐ visit all the continents
- ☐ cross a country on public transport
- ☐ fly in a hot-air balloon
- ☐ learn another language
- ☐ do a bungee jump
- ☐ learn to ski
- ☐ learn to scuba dive

- ☐ learn to dance the tango
- ☐ do volunteer work
- ☐ climb a volcano
- ☐ learn how to make a national dish
- ☐ eat something exotic
- ☐ attend a music festival
- ☐ visit the birthplace of an important person

B Look at these example sentences from the text. Which word introduces a consequence? Which word introduces a reason? Find and <u>underline</u> other sentences in the text which explain a reason or a consequence.

I like to plan my life, so I made a list …
I didn't learn a foreign language … because I chose to study art.

Over to You

C Make a list of things that you are going to do in the next ten years.

_____

_____

_____

_____

_____

D ✎ Choose five things from your list in Exercise C and, in your notebook, write a short text about why you are going to do each thing.

WRITING TUTOR

I'm interested in … so …
I like … because/so …
I want to … so …
I'm going to … because …
Now, / Next year, / In two years, I'm going to …

DOWN TIME

Do the trivia quiz. Choose the correct answer.

1 Who married Javier Bardem in 2010?
   a) Salma Hayek
   b) Penélope Cruz
   c) Scarlett Johansson

2 Which nationality was Mozart?
   a) Austrian
   b) German
   c) Russian

3 In which year did the modern Olympics® begin?
   a) 1876
   b) 1886
   c) 1896

4 Where were the 2008 Olympic® Games held?
   a) Great Britain
   b) South Africa
   c) China

5 Which famous singer worked at Dunkin' Donuts?
   a) Madonna
   b) Taylor Swift
   c) Pink

6 Who wrote the *Twilight* series?
   a) JK Rowling
   b) Robert Pattinson
   c) Stephenie Meyer

7 Which film didn't win an Academy Award® for best film?
   a) *The Artist*
   b) *Midnight in Paris*
   c) *The King's Speech*

8 Which female artist had a hit with the song 'Umbrella'?
   a) Beyoncé
   b) Rihanna
   c) Katy Perry

9 Which is the most successful album of all time?
   a) Pink Floyd: *The Wall*
   b) Michael Jackson: *Thriller*
   c) The Beatles: *The White Album*

10 Where did Usain Bolt run the fastest 100 m?
   a) Beijing
   b) London
   c) Paris

11 Where was Ricky Martin born?
   a) Mexico
   b) Cuba
   c) Puerto Rico

12 Which country founded New Orleans?
   a) Spain
   b) France
   c) Belgium

Audioscript

UNIT 1

Track 01

1 Can you spell that?
2 Can you speak more slowly?
3 How do you say that in English?
4 Can you repeat that, please?
5 What does that mean?
6 Can you help me?

Track 02

Receptionist: Excuse me, can you spell your surname, please?
Ms Cardoza: Yes, it's C-A-R-D-O-Z-A.
Receptionist: Thank you. And what's your phone number?
Ms Cardoza: It's 01743 214091.
Receptionist: OK. You're in room 235. Here's your room key.
Ms Cardoza: Thanks.
Receptionist: You're welcome. Enjoy your stay.

Track 03

1 My birthday is on the ninth of October.
2 This is my first day in this class.
3 Next Wednesday is the twenty-fifth of November.
4 The last day of August is the thirty-first.
5 My birthday is April the seventeenth.
6 Today is the twelfth.

Track 04

Hi, my name is Lucy Cheng. My surname is Cheng. That's C-H-E-N-G. I'm from Taipei in Taiwan. I'm 20 years old. I would like to know some information about your English course. Can you please call me back? My number is 01555 841078. That's 01555 841078. Thank you.

Track 05

A: Barton University. Can I help you?
B: Yes, hello. I want to take an evening class, please.
A: OK. First I need to take some information. What is your first name, please?
B: Jane. My name is Jane.
A: And what is your surname?
B: It's Robinson.
A: Can you spell that?
B: R-O-B-I-N-S-O-N.
A: And how old are you, Jane?
B: I'm 19.
A: When is your birthday?
B: In December, the seventh of December.
A: Can you repeat that?
B: Of course, it's the seventh of December.
A: OK. And finally, what's your email address?
B: It's jane192@mail.com.
A: Great. So what class do you want to take?

UNIT 2

Track 06

Which occupations are interesting? Hmm … I think being a doctor is very interesting. You can help people. You can discover new medicines. That's my number 1. And number 2 is 'engineer'. Being an engineer is interesting because you can build new things like bridges and tunnels. I think 'firefighter' is my number 3. It's exciting but very dangerous. I don't like this job. I think 'police officer' is number 4 because it's hard work and dangerous. It's not a lot of fun. And my number 5 is 'taxi driver' because driving a taxi is not interesting. But my number 6 is 'writer'. You don't talk to anyone. You just stay on the computer all day. So, yes, 1 doctor, 2 engineer, 3 firefighter, 4 police officer, 5 taxi driver and 6 writer.

Track 07

This is my family tree. That's me on the end. My name is Angela. And there's my mum and my dad. My mum is Sheila, and my dad is Frank. That's my sister. Her name is Kate. She's married. That's her husband, Leo, and their two children, Emma and Lucy – Lucy is on the right. Mike is my brother. He isn't married. Oh, yes, and the most important person – that's my grandma, Mary.

Track 08

Brenda Jones is a lawyer. She lives in Manchester. Brenda starts work at 8.30am. She thinks her job is very exciting. Her husband isn't a lawyer. He's an engineer. Their daughter is a student.

UNIT 3

Track 09

A: Hi, Bettina. Can I ask you some questions for a survey?
B: Sure! Go ahead.
A: Do you listen to music?
B: Yes, I do. I listen to folk music. I really like folk music.
A: And do you play the guitar?
B: No, I don't.
A: Do your parents listen to music a lot?
B: No, they don't.
A: Do you buy a lot of CDs?
B: No, I don't. I buy MP3s online.
A: Great! That's all. Thanks a lot!
B: Sure, no problem.

Track 10

1 Everyone likes Marisa because she tells lots of good jokes and makes them laugh.
2 Lucy doesn't like big parties with lots of people. She is nervous about meeting new people. She prefers going out with just one or two friends.
3 Eddie likes to meet new people. He likes to talk to people and he isn't shy.
4 Simon is a kind person. He opens doors and helps people with their bags.
5 Clare is a good friend. When life is difficult, she's always there to help you.
6 Andy is good fun and has lots of friends – everyone likes him.

Track 11

Interviewer:	Today, I have Alex Hartford and his sister Jenny in the studio. You know them as brother and sister pop group Generation Y. Alex and Jenny, welcome.
Alex/Jenny:	Thanks.
Interviewer:	So, we know about your music, but tell us a little about you. Are you similar?
Alex:	No way! We're very different. I'm a shy guy. I don't really have a lot of friends – well, I have a few good friends, but that's it.
Interviewer:	And what about you, Jenny?
Jenny:	I'm the party animal in our family!
Alex:	Yeah, she's really sociable and popular. She likes to meet new people, and everybody likes her.
Jenny:	But you're so funny, Alex. The jokes you tell make me laugh a lot!
Interviewer:	OK! And tell us a little about your daily life.
Alex:	Well, we're musicians, so every morning we go to our studio to write new songs. After we finish, I usually practise my guitar.
Jenny:	And I usually go to the gym to do exercise in the afternoon.
Interviewer:	And what do you do in your free time? Do you do the same things?
Jenny:	Not at all. At the weekend, I like to see friends and go to parties.
Alex:	I like to see my friends, but we don't go to parties. We usually do something quiet like go bowling or watch a film.
Interviewer:	Sounds like a great life! Well thanks, Alex and Jenny.

UNIT 4

Track 12

1 Hurry up, it's twenty past eight.
2 It's nine o'clock on Tuesday, 22nd August.
3 A: What time is it, please?
  B: It's quarter past six.
4 The time is eleven forty-five pm.
5 Come on, it's five thirty. Time to go home!
6 It's seven fifteen, wake up!

Track 13

Hi. My name is Sarah. I'm a fashion designer. On Mondays, I usually go to the design studio and give them my designs. The rest of the week I work at home. On Tuesday mornings, I do exercise in the gym. On Wednesday evenings, I look after my sister's children. She goes to an evening class to study computing.
On Thursday evenings, I usually invite my friends for dinner. I always go dancing on Friday nights. On Saturdays, I go shopping and on Sundays, I ride my bike.

Track 14

Hi. My name is Francisco. I'm a computer programmer. On Mondays, I usually stay at home and work online. The rest of the week I work in the office. On Tuesday mornings, I go swimming. On Wednesday evenings, I go to an evening class. On Thursday evenings, I usually visit my parents for dinner. On Friday evenings, I go to the cinema. On Saturdays, I go for a walk in the park and on Sundays, I go shopping.

UNIT 5

Track 15

A: So, what places can we visit when I come to see you tomorrow?
B: We can go to the art gallery and the museum, that's for sure. They're both really interesting. How about shopping? Do you want to go to the shopping centre?
A: No! I hate shopping centres. I want to go for a walk in the park and then maybe go to a café for lunch.
B: OK. That sounds great. We can have lunch in the museum – the café there is really good – and then go for a walk in the park.
A: Great!

Track 16

1 A: Excuse me, where's the museum?
  B: Go straight ahead and take the second left.
  A: I see. Straight ahead and take the third left?
  B: No, not the third left, the second left.
  A: Thanks.
  B: No problem.
2 A: Excuse me, how do I get to the shopping centre?
  B: Take the first right. Then go straight ahead.
  A: First left. Then go straight ahead?
  B: No, first right, then go straight ahead.
  A: Thank you.
  B: You're welcome.
3 A: Excuse me, how do I get to the train station?
  B: Turn left here and then take the third right.
  A: Go straight here and then take the third right?
  B: No, turn left here and then take the third right.
  A: OK. Thanks.

Track 17

Edinburgh, the capital of Scotland, is a fascinating city. Stay in the old part of town, and visit its beautiful buildings and historical monuments. There are many castles in Scotland, but don't miss Edinburgh Castle because there you can learn about Scottish kings and queens, and see the crown jewels. At night, try the walking tour. This way you can visit famous places from the *Harry Potter* films. It starts at 10pm in the cemetery. Don't forget your camera and bring warm clothes. In August, there is a famous international arts event. It's called the Edinburgh Festival. There are comedy, dance, music and theatre shows all day and night. Remember to book a hotel early because there are over one million visitors during that month.

UNIT 6

Track 18

1	exciting	3	relaxing	5	boring
2	stressful	4	unhealthy	6	green

Track 19

My younger sister Donna eats a lot of fast food. She watches TV all day and doesn't do any exercise.
My brother Mark travels all over the world for his job. And he meets lots of famous people.
My brother's wife Karen eats only organic fruit and vegetables. She rides a bike to work every day.
My dad never worries about anything. He likes to read and listen to music, and he always has time to talk to his children.
My mum works in a bank. She works late every night and is always worried about her work.
And me … well, I go to university, I come home, I study, I watch TV. Every day is the same old routine, really. My lifestyle isn't very exciting!

Track 20

1 I am twenty-nine years old.
2 The time is five past four.
3 My phone number is zero one two one two, three one nine five seven eight.
4 This building dates from nineteen forty-nine.
5 My date of birth is the seventeenth of April, nineteen ninety-six.

Track 21

Hi. My name is Leonardo Oliveira. My account number is 5421390426. My ID number is 11488566. I'm calling about this month's statement, which is £556. There's a £59 charge, but I don't know what it's for. Please call me back. My number is 01559 431323.

UNIT 7

Track 22

1 Elena can play the piano.
2 Peter can dance.
3 I can't sing.
4 We can't drive.

Track 23

A: Ricky, can you help me with this questionnaire?
B: Sure.
A: Can you play a sport?
B: Yes, I can play tennis. Can you?
A: No, I'm not good at sport. Can you speak another language?
B: Yes, I can. I can speak German.
A: Oh! I can speak German, too. Can you cook?
B: Yes, I can. I can cook spaghetti. Very delicious.
A: Mm, yum. That sounds great because I can't cook anything. How about some spaghetti for dinner tonight?

Track 24

Chloe is very talented. She can play all kinds of musical instruments, including the piano. She's also good at singing and can sing opera as well as traditional songs.
Alicia is good at all kinds of sports. Her favourite sports are karate and football. She's also good at dancing, especially salsa.
Tony is good at languages. He can speak Russian and German. And he can also cook Russian food.

Track 25

1 A: Can you play any musical instruments?
  B: Yes, I can play the guitar and the piano.
  A: Wow. That's amazing!
2 B: Can you speak any foreign languages?
  A: Yes, I can speak Esperanto.
  B: Oh, really?
3 A: Can you dance?
  B: No, but I can sing.
  A: Oh, that's great.

Track 26

1 Hi, I'm Sara. I love music. I'm friendly and generous. I can play the guitar and I can sing.
2 Um, hi, I'm Dominic. Um, I'm clever and honest. I can speak English and French. I can play chess. I like reading and doing quiet activities.
3 My name's Brianna. I'm very patient and reliable. I can cook very well and can make delicious sushi. I like doing new things.
4 Hi. I'm Dean. I'm very athletic and I like sport. I can play basketball very well. I like doing exciting things.

UNIT 8

Track 27

1 A: Can I help you?
  B: Yes. How much is that jumper?
  A: It's £29.95.
2 A: Excuse me. How much are those shoes?
  B: They're £85.
3 A: Are these T-shirts £5?
  B: Well, usually they are, but today they're on sale for only £4.50 each.
4 A: Excuse me. How much is this shirt?
  B: It's £19.50.
  A: Thank you.

Track 28

A: Hello and welcome to *Guess the Price!* We show you things, and you have to guess the price. The contestant with the closest guess wins the item! First, we have this great compact refrigerator.
B: Hmm, I think it's £199.
C: I think it's more. I say £250.
D: I don't think it's very expensive. How about £130?
A: OK, well, the real price is … £150! So you win, number three. Congratulations! Our next item is this amazing TV. How much is it?
B: I say £399.
C: Oh, no, I think it's £350.
D: I think it's more expensive. £500?
A: And the real price is … £350! So you win, number two. Congratulations! Our next item is this beautiful necklace. How much is it?
B: My guess is £1,000.
C: I say, hmm, £1,500.
D: I think it's £2,000.
A: And the real price is … £1,000! So you win, number one. Congratulations! See you again next week on *Guess the Price!*

Track 29

1	expensive	3	versatile	5	user-friendly
2	compact	4	powerful		

Track 30

1 You can use this to send emails and messages, listen to music, surf the internet – and a lot of other things.

2 This is a luxury product. It isn't cheap, but the sound quality is excellent.

3 This player is so easy to use! You won't believe how great it is.

4 You can put this in your shirt pocket. It's less than seven centimetres wide and weighs just a hundred grams.

5 This version has a bigger memory and a higher speed connection than our previous model.

UNIT 9

Track 31

A: Good afternoon. Could I speak to Mr Brown, please?

B: I'm sorry. He isn't here at the moment. Would you like to leave a message?

A: Yes, please. Could you ask him to call me back? My name's Mike Thompson, and my number is 01460 013192.

B: Yes, of course.

A: Thank you.

B: You're welcome.

Track 32

A: Are you ready to order?

B: Dan, do you know what you want to eat?

C: Yes … um, what is the soup of the day?

A: It's tomato soup.

C: OK. I'd like the tomato soup and then I'd like the grilled fish with potatoes, please.

A: Certainly. And what would you like to order, madam?

B: I want the soup of the day, too, please. And after that I'd like to have the roast chicken with vegetables and … yes, I'd like cake for dessert and a coffee.

A: And what would you like for dessert, sir?

C: Hmm, just coffee for me, please.

A: Thank you. I'll be right back with your order.

Track 33

A: Good morning and welcome to *Healthy Eating*. Today we have chef Antonio Mereda with us. Welcome to the show.

B: Thank you. It's a pleasure to be here.

A: So, what do you want to make today?

B: Well, today, Michaela, I'd like to make my favourite dish: spinach and strawberry salad.

A: Wow, that sounds unusual. What do you need for it?

B: Well, you need some spinach and a few strawberries, of course. You also need some nuts and some butter. And for the dressing you need oil, vinegar, paprika and onion.

A: OK. And how do you make it?

B: First, you melt the butter over a medium heat, then add the nuts. You need to cook these for about one minute. Put the spinach, strawberries and nuts in a bowl. Combine the oil, vinegar, paprika and onion, and pour this over the salad.

A: Sounds fantastic! Well, thank you to Antonio.

UNIT 10

Track 34

A: What did you do on Friday night?

B: I went out for dinner.

A: Where did you go?

B: To the new Thai restaurant. It's fantastic.

A: Oh, wow! Did you have a good time?

B: Yes, it was great.

A: Who did you go with?

B: With my girlfriend.

A: And how was the food?

B: Oh, fantastic. I love Thai food.

A: And was it very expensive?

B: Mmm. Not too bad, actually.

Track 35

1 A: So, how was your exam, Sarah?

B: Oh, it was OK, you know …

A: Not too good, huh?

B: Well, the first few questions were OK, but then I got confused.

A: Was it more difficult than you thought?

B: Everyone said the exam was very hard. I'm sure I failed.

A: Well, better luck next time.

B: Thanks!

2 A: Hey, Andy, how was your trip?

B: Amazing! We had a really good time.

A: Were you in the mountains?

B: Yes, there was a lot of snow. It was great!

A: Did you go out on the slopes every day?

B: Yes, we did. And I only fell over twice!

A: Sounds like a good trip!

3 A: Simon, how's it going?

B: Not bad, how about you?

A: Great! How was the match?

B: Oh, I'm exhausted. I stayed up all night. We were celebrating.

A: Oh, so you won?

B: You bet! Two-nil!

A: Sounds like it was a good match.

B: Yes, you should come and watch next time. I can get some tickets for you.

A: Cool! I'd like that!

UNIT 11

Track 36

Isabel Allende was born in Lima, Peru in 1942, but she grew up in Chile. After she left school in 1958, she worked as a translator, TV presenter and journalist in Europe. She got married in 1962 and she had her first child, Paula, in 1963. In 1966, Allende returned to Chile, and she had her second child, Nicolás, there that year. In 1975, she moved to Venezuela where she got a job as a journalist. In 1982, she published her first novel, *The House of the Spirits*. Now her novels are famous all over the world, and she is head of a foundation to help protect the rights of women and children. In 2003, she became a US citizen and she now lives in California.

Track 37

A: Mike, do you want to try this literary quiz?
B: Well, I'm not good at literature, but why not … go ahead.
A: OK, question one. Who wrote *The Merchant of Venice*?
B: Oh, yeah. That's easy – Shakespeare!
A: Yes, that's right. And who wrote *The Old Man and the Sea*?
B: Just a second. Um, was it Hemingway?
A: Correct! And how many books are there in the *Harry Potter* series?
B: Um, I'm not sure but … I think there are six.
A: No, seven! And what's the name of the main character in *Twilight*?
B: Let me think, um, hmm, I can't remember.
A: It's Bella.

Track 38

Hello, everyone! Today we have a great film to recommend, called *Becoming Jane*. It's a film about the life of the English author Jane Austen.

Jane Austen was born in 1775, at a time when women got married to help their family and didn't usually get jobs or earn money. The story in the film starts when Jane was a young woman and started writing, but also at a time when her family wanted her to get married. Her mother wanted her to marry a rich man. But Jane fell in love with a poor lawyer. The story is about their romance and the dilemma they faced.

I loved this film as it was both romantic and sad. I say go out and rent it today!

UNIT 12

Track 39

A: Hi, Jim. How's it going?
B: Great! I'm going on holiday tomorrow.
A: That's nice! Where are you going?
B: First, I'm flying to Kenya with a group of friends.
A: Flying to Kenya! That's a long trip!
B: Yeah, we're going on a wildlife adventure trip – we're going up into the forests to see wild animals like gorillas and chimpanzees.
A: What kind of holiday is that? It sounds tiring … and dangerous!
B: Yes … That's my ideal holiday – an adventure trip, exploring unusual and exciting places far away from civilisation.
A: OK …, but I prefer staying in a luxury hotel on a beach! Adventure trips are not really my thing.

Track 40

1 A: Is that your new bike? It looks great!
  B: Yes, I can't wait to try it out.
  A: OK. Let's go this weekend.
2 A: I really need some new shoes.
  B: I think there's a sale on this Saturday.
  A: Great! Do you want to come with me?
3 A: Aren't you going in? The water's really warm!
  B: No, you go in. I'll lie here on the beach for a while.
  A: Go on, come in with me!
  B: Oh, OK then.
4 A: I'd like to go with you, but my leg hurts.
  B: We're only going around the park for about half an hour and we can go slowly if you want.
  A: OK. Hang on. I'll get my trainers.

Track 41

A: What resolutions are you going to make for next year, Toshi?
B: Um … well … I'm not very good at making resolutions, Pete, but … I'm definitely going to start bringing a packed lunch to work. I'm going to stop eating junk food like pizza and crisps.
A: Good idea! I know what mine's going to be: I'm going to start cycling to work every day. It's healthy, and I could lose some weight, too. And I'm going to stop eating chocolate.
B: Now that's a resolution I couldn't keep. I love chocolate. But I'm going to stop drinking coffee. I'm going to start drinking green tea instead. It's healthier.
A: Green tea! Good idea. I'm going to do that, too.

Answer key

UNIT 1

Section 1
Exercise A
Possible answers:
My <u>name</u> is Hilda Gonzalez. I'm a <u>student</u> at Bristol <u>University</u>. I study <u>English</u> and <u>medicine</u>.
I have a part-time job in a <u>pharmacy</u>. My interests are <u>literature</u>, <u>music</u>, films and <u>badminton</u>. I love animals, especially horses. My best friend is Ayako Kubota. We are in the same English <u>class</u>. Our teacher is Mr Mason.

Exercise B
1 c 2 d 3 f 4 a 5 b 6 e

Section 2
Exercise A
1 spell 2 speak 3 say 4 repeat
5 mean 6 help

Exercise B
1 Can you spell that?
2 Can you repeat that, please?
3 What does that mean?
4 Can you speak more slowly?
5 How do you say that in English?
6 Can you help me?

Section 3
Exercise A
1 is 2 Are 3 isn't 4 Are 5 am
6 is

Exercise B
1 is 2 isn't 3 am 4 are
5 Is; isn't 6 Are; are 7 Are; 'm not
8 Are; aren't 9 is

What's right?
She is 25 years old.

Exercise C
1 'm 2 'm 3 's 4 'm 5 's 6 Are
7 'm not 8 'm 9 Is 10 isn't 11 's
12 Are 13 am 14 're

Section 4
Exercise A
1 Excuse me 2 please 3 Thank you / Thanks 4 Thanks / Thank you
5 You're welcome

Exercise B
1 Excuse me 2 please 3 You're welcome.

Section 5
Exercise A
1 9th 3 25th 5 17th
2 1st 4 31st 6 12th

Exercise B
1 ninth 4 thirty-first
2 first 5 seventeenth
3 twenty-fifth 6 twelfth

Exercise C
1 27th 2 11th 3 13th 4 22nd
5 4th 6 30th

Section 6
Exercise A
1 Where 2 What 3 How 4 When

Exercise B
First name: Lucy
Surname: Cheng
Country: Taiwan
Age: 20
Telephone number: 01555 841078

What's right?
Where are you from?

Exercise C
1 What is (What's); Lucy
2 What is (What's) her surname?; Cheng
3 Where is (Where's) she from?; Taiwan
4 How old is she?; 20
5 What is (What's); 01555 841078

Listen and write
Exercise A
First name: Jane
Surname: Robinson
Age: 19
Birthday: 7th Dec
Email: jane192@mail.com

Down Time
Exercise A
seventeenth, first, seventh, fourth, fifth, tenth, second, third, fifteenth

Exercise B
1 is 2 eighth 3 speak 4 help
5 old 6 mean 7 spell
Letters in circles: 1 i 2 g 3 e 4 h
5 l 6 n 7 s

Exercise C
English

Exercise D
A: Where are you from?
B: I'm from Madrid. And you?
A: I'm from Rome. My name's Paolo.
B: Nice to meet you. I'm Sonia.

UNIT 2

Section 1
Exercise A
1 doctor; D 4 engineer; F
2 firefighter; B 5 police officer; C
3 taxi driver; A 6 writer; E

Exercise B
1 doctor 2 engineer 3 firefighter
4 police officer 5 taxi driver 6 writer

Section 2
Exercise A
a: musician, teacher, singer
an: artist, engineer, actor
– (no article): writers, students, lawyers

Exercise B
1 an 3 – 5 –; The
2 the 4 the

Exercise C
1 Are you <u>a</u> teacher?
2 They <u>are doctors</u> in the health service.
3 My brother is a docto<u>r</u>.
4 Is Dave <u>a</u> lawyer?
5 I am not <u>a</u> student.
6 My brother is <u>a</u> teacher in a school. <u>The</u> school is in Brighton.

What's right?
He is a musician.

Section 3
Exercise A
1 Mary 2 Sheila 3 Frank 4 Leo
5 Kate 6 Mike 7 Emma 8 Lucy

Exercise B
1 grandma 2 parents 3 brother
4 sister 5 Leo 6 Emma/Lucy
7 Emma/Lucy 8 grandparents

Section 4
Exercise A
1 c 2 b 3 d 4 a 5 e 6 f

Exercise B
1 Jones 2 Manchester 3 8.30am
4 exciting 5 engineer 6 daughter

Section 5
Exercise A
1 's got; hasn't got
2 hasn't got; 's got
3 haven't got; 've got
4 've got; haven't got

Exercise B
1 sister's 2 children's 3 Tom's
4 mother's 5 grandparents'
6 parents'

What's right?
My cat's name is Tippy.

Exercise C
1 Hers 2 mine 3 theirs
4 ours; yours 5 his 6 Hers; his

Section 6
Exercise A
1 f; My birthday is in <u>N</u>ovember.
2 b; We are from <u>P</u>eru.
3 a; They study <u>E</u>nglish.
4 g; My sister and <u>I</u> are doctors.
5 c; My teacher is Mr <u>D</u>aniels.
6 h; <u>I</u>t is five o'clock.
7 d; Antonia lives in <u>R</u>ome.
8 e; Your class is on <u>W</u>ednesday.

Exercise B
1 My sister Alison is a writer.
2 She writes short stories and books for children.
3 Her job is very interesting, but it is also difficult.
4 She sometimes travels around the country and talks about her work.
5 Her books are very popular with children and adults.
6 She's got two awards for best children's books of the year.

Read and write

Exercise A

He's a sound engineer.

Exercise B

1 33.
2 Yes, he is, because he listens to great bands from all over the world and he meets famous musicians.
3 No, it isn't.
4 Alan.
5 She's a piano teacher.

Exercise C

1 Name
2 Relationship
3 Age
4 Job
5 Nationality
6 Lives
7 Other information
8 Opinion about job
9 Family

Down Time

Exercise A

grandparents
1 Eleanor   2 Richard   3 Edward
4 Annette   5 Lauren   6 Brenda
7 Mike   8 Sam   9 Susan   10 Tim
11 Andrew   12 Rick   13 Clare
14 Sara/Sophie   15 Sara/Sophie
16 Naomi

Exercise B

singer, software engineer, lawyer, artist, firefighter, police officer, soldier, taxi driver, architect, journalist, doctor

Exercise C

well-paid, interesting work, good salary, hard-working, job security

UNIT 3

Section 1

Exercise A

1 listens
2 doesn't watch; doesn't read
3 Does; play; No; doesn't
4 Do; buy; Yes; do
5 Does; read; No; doesn't

Exercise B

1 likes   2 doesn't play   3 don't listen
4 buys

What's right?

Does he read books? Yes, he does.

Exercise C

1 Do you listen   2 do you play
3 Do your parents listen
4 Do you buy   5 buy

Section 2

Exercise A

Possible answers:

mystery, collection, puzzles, solution, detectives, fantasy, novels, series, characters, biographies, historical, real, fantasies, romantic

Exercise B

1 Leo   2 Danni   3 Leo   4 Monika
5 Suzie; Danni

Section 3

Exercise A

1 b   2 g   3 e   4 f   5 h   6 d   7 c
8 a

Exercise B

1 go to the cinema   4 go bowling
2 play sport   5 listen to music
3 do exercise   6 watch TV

Section 4

Exercise A

1 d   2 e   3 b   4 f   5 c   6 a

Exercise B

1 What   2 Why   3 When   4 Who
5 Where

Exercise C

1 What does Tony like to do in his free time?
2 Who does Tony play football with?
3 When does Tony play football?
4 Where does Tony play football?
5 Why does Tony like football?

What's right?

What does he do in his free time?

Section 5

1 What do you; d
2 How about; c
3 What's your; a
4 Do you; b

Section 6

Exercise A

1 funny   2 shy   3 sociable
4 considerate   5 loyal   6 popular

Exercise B

1 shy   2 confident   3 popular
4 funny   5 extrovert   6 loyal
7 introvert   8 sociable

Listen and write

Exercise A

their personality, their daily activities, their free-time activities, their friends

Exercise B

1 A   2 J   3 J   4 A
write new songs: A/J
go bowling: A
see friends: A/J
go to parties: J
watch a film: A
do exercise at the gym: J
practise the guitar: A

Exercise C

1 sociable   2 confident
3 independent   4 popular   5 funny
6 shy   7 considerate/loyal
8 loyal/considerate

Down Time

Exercise A

1 go online   5 listen to music
2 go bowling   6 watch TV
3 play tennis   7 go to the cinema
4 play video games

Exercise B

1 funny   5 popular
2 sociable   6 friends
3 confident   7 extroverts
4 shy   8 introverts

UNIT 4

Section 1

Exercise A

1   2

3   4

5   6

Exercise B

1 It's eight twenty. / It's twenty past eight.
2 It's nine o'clock.
3 It's quarter past six. / It's six fifteen.
4 It's eleven forty-five. / It's quarter to twelve.
5 It's five thirty. / It's half past five.
6 It's seven fifteen. / It's quarter past seven.

Section 2

Exercise A

1 always   2 usually   3 often
4 sometimes   5 rarely   6 never

Exercise B

1 We are always at home in the evening.
2 Frank and Emilia have dinner in a restaurant once a week.
3 Yolanda rarely watches TV.
4 My brother is often online in the morning.
5 Hector never has any free time.
6 Clare drives to work three times a week.

What's right?

He is never late.

Exercise C

1 Suzanna always takes the bus.
2 Frank and Liz often go to the cinema.
3 Matt always goes swimming in his lunch break.
4 Marie rarely eats in a restaurant.
5 We usually drive to work.
6 Leona is sometimes absent.
7 Toby never gets up early on Sundays.

Section 3

Exercise A

1 b   2 d   3 a   4 c   5 g   6 f   7 e

Exercises B and C

Hi. My name is Francisco. I'm a computer programmer. On Mondays, I usually stay at home and work online. The rest of the week I work in the office. On Tuesday mornings, I go swimming. On Wednesday evenings, I go to an evening class. On Thursday evenings, I usually visit my parents for dinner. On Friday evenings, I go to the cinema. On Saturdays, I go for a walk in the park and on Sundays, I go shopping.

Section 4

Exercise A

on: Wednesday, weekdays
at: four o'clock, midnight, night, the weekend
in: the afternoon, the evening, the morning

Exercise B

1 on 2 in 3 at 4 in 5 at 6 on

Exercise C

He gets up. He has a shower. He eats breakfast. He reads the newspaper. He goes to work. He goes to the park. He eats lunch. He reads the newspaper. He goes to the shop. He goes back to the office. He finishes work. He goes home. He watches the news. He has dinner. He reads a book. He goes to bed.

Section 5

Exercise A

1 a 2 a 3 b 4 b

Exercise B

1 go to the cinema after we go shopping
2 goes to the library before he goes to his English class
3 children watch TV until we have dinner
4 practise the piano until it is eight o'clock
5 Zach and Mina cook dinner, they watch TV
6 Becky has lunch, she goes to the gym

What's right?

He has a shower after he has breakfast.

Section 6

Exercise A

1 Toshihiko (starts) work at seven thirty.
2 It (is) sunny and warm today.
3 Emil and Renata (go) to the gym on Saturdays.
4 My brother (has) a very interesting job. He (is) a travel writer.
5 We (buy) music online. We rarely (buy) CDs from a shop.
6 It (s) five o'clock.

Exercise B

Adam usually finishes work at 5.30pm. After work, he goes to his English class. His class finishes at 7pm. Before he goes home, he goes to a café with his friends. Adam gets home at around 8.30pm. After dinner, he does his homework until it is time to go to sleep.

Read and write

Exercise A

usually, rarely, often, always, usually, sometimes, never, sometimes

Exercise B

8am – Phoebe starts work.
8.30 – She has a staff meeting.
9.30 – She answers emails.
12pm – She works on new projects.
2pm – She has lunch.
3pm – She has meetings with clients.
8pm – She finishes work.
9pm – She arrives home and cooks dinner.
10pm – She watches TV or reads professional magazines.

Down Time

Exercise A

Across:

1 sociable   4 go for a walk
2 always   5 rarely
3 boring

Down:

1 one thirty   5 noon
2 online   6 loyal
3 an   7 before
4 Saturday   8 work

Exercise B

1 Time waits for no man.
2 Time flies when you are having fun.
3 The early bird catches the worm.

UNIT 5

Section 1

Exercise A

1 is 2 are 3 is 4 aren't 5 aren't

Exercise B

1 aren't 2 is 3 Are 4 many
5 any 6 Are 7 several 8 are

What's right?

There are a lot of festivals.

Section 2

Exercise A

1 cinema 2 museum
3 shopping centre 4 art gallery
5 park 6 zoo

Exercise B

Students should tick the following: art gallery, park, café, museum

Exercise C

1 shopping centre 2 bus station
3 chocolate factory 4 cinema

Section 3

Exercise A

Blog 1 c
Blog 2 a
Blog 3 b

Exercise B

1 positive

Parrot Jungle Island is amazing. The gardens are beautiful, and there are thousands of exotic animals and plants. There's lots of stuff to do – take photos, watch the animal shows or relax on the private beach. It's in the heart of Miami, and there's a good bus service. A fantastic day out for the whole family.

2 positive

The Casa Bella is great! Real luxury! The rooms are large and comfortable. There's a bar right next to the pool with beautiful palm trees and umbrellas. The service is excellent. And it's five minutes from the beach!

3 negative

Don't go to Miami Grill! There isn't any seating outside, and inside it's too hot and not very clean. The service is terrible – the waiters are not helpful. The food isn't great, and the drinks are too expensive.

Section 4

Exercise A

Richard: Excuse me. How do I get to the underground station?
Amelia: Go straight ahead and take the second right onto Oxford Street. Then turn left onto Green Avenue and walk for about 200 metres. Don't cross the street. The underground station is there on the left. Don't worry. It's easy to find!
Richard: Thank you very much.

Exercise B

1 give   6 Don't forget
2 Visit   7 Don't stay
3 have/drink   8 Take
4 Eat   9 Walk
5 drink/have   10 Don't go

What's right?

Don't forget your umbrella.

Exercise C

1 Don't visit New York in the winter.
2 Go to some shows on Broadway.
3 Don't take a taxi – they're expensive!
4 Buy some designer clothes and shoes.
5 Don't spend too much money!
6 Take a ride around Central Park.

Section 5

Exercise A

police station

Exercise B

1 fountain 2 park 3 bus station
4 art gallery

Exercise C

Start at the zoo on River Street. Go over the bridge and straight ahead. Turn left and go straight ahead. Take the second left. The café is on the left, on Park Avenue, opposite the park.

Section 6
Exercise A
A: Excuse me, how do I get to the library?
B: First, turn left here and then take the first street on the right.
A: Turn left. Then take the first street on the left.
B: No, the first street on the right.
A: Ah! First street on the right. OK, thanks.

Exercise B
1 Go straight ahead and take the second left.
2 Take the first right. Then go straight ahead.
3 Turn left here and then take the third right.

Listen and write
Exercise A
1 fascinating　　5 August
2 buildings　　6 comedy
3 walking tour　　7 book a hotel
4 10pm　　8 one million

Exercise B
1 fascinating (Edinburgh), old (part of town), beautiful (buildings), historical (monuments), famous (places from the *Harry Potter* films), warm (clothes), famous (arts event), international (arts event)
2 because there you can learn about Scottish kings and queens, and see the crown jewels. This way you can visit famous places ... because there are over one million visitors during that month; because ..., This way ...

Down Time
Exercise A
Red Square, San Diego Zoo, Central Park, Guggenheim Museum, Trevi Fountain

Exercise B

H	E	R	P	E	T	H	E	B	O
N	R	E	A	A	N	D	I	G	E
E	M	O	R	V	R	L	E	E	R
W	Y	W	H	E	B	I	R	E	N
Y	B	K	Q	A	D	K	S	N	K
O	W	T	O	N	V	Z	L	F	M
R	T	L	A	H	L	F	Q	M	B
K	T	S	T	M	O	S	C	O	W

UNIT 6

Section 1
Exercise A
1 exciting　2 stressful　3 relaxing
4 unhealthy　5 boring　6 green

Exercise B
1 stressful　2 relaxing
3 green　4 exciting　5 unhealthy
6 boring

Section 2
Exercise A
Add -*ing*: happening, studying, talking, waiting
Drop *e* and add -*ing*: having, living, taking, writing
Double final consonant and add -*ing*: planning, running, swimming, winning

Exercise B
1 is reading　　4 is listening
2 are talking　　5 is standing
3 are drinking

Exercise C
1 In picture 1, the boy is playing with a dog, but in picture 2, he is eating ice cream.
2 In picture 1, the girl is using a tablet, but in picture 2, she is reading a magazine.
3 In picture 1, the man is listening to music, but in picture 2, he is playing the guitar.
4 In picture 1, the woman is feeding the birds, but in picture 2, she is playing with a dog.
5 In picture 1, the students are having a picnic, but in picture 2, they are eating ice cream.

What's right?
The boy is playing with a dog.

Section 3
Exercise A
1 29
2 4.05
3 01212 319578
4 1949
5 17/04/1996

Exercise B
Name: Leonardo Oliveira
Account number: 5421390426
ID number: 11488566
Amount on statement: £556
Problem: there's a £59 charge
Telephone number: 01559 431323

Section 4
Exercise A
1 e　2 a　3 f　4 b　5 d　6 c
Exercise B
1 reuse　2 get　3 save　4 pick; up
5 turn off　6 organic

Section 5
Exercise A
1 do you do; write
2 is he going; is going
3 do they have
4 Does she like; don't know

Exercise B
1 I am studying now. I have an exam tomorrow.
2 Albert is working very hard on his project. He needs to finish it today.
3 Raoul usually plays squash three times a week. He wants to have a healthy lifestyle.
4 Kirsty doesn't know Ben. They aren't friends.

What's right?
I love you.
Exercise C
1 are; doing　2 am studying　3 am taking　4 Do; like　5 want　6 play
7 am working　8 like

Section 6
Exercise A
1 object　2 verb　3 subject
4 object　5 subject　6 verb

Exercise B
1 verb　2 object　3 object　4 verb
5 subject　6 verb

Exercise C
1 walk　2 newspapers　3 energy
4 use　5 My neighbour　6 turn off

Read and write
Exercise A
planting trees, informing people about ecological problems, cycling, using public transport, selling local food, picking up the litter, save water, recycle bottles and paper

Down Time
Exercise B
1 save　2 turn off　3 reuse
4 recycle　5 get　6 pick up

U	S	E	A	B	R	C
D	E	P	F	G	E	T
G	S	I	N	V	C	U
H	A	C	O	W	Y	R
I	V	K	P	X	C	N
R	E	U	S	E	L	O
J	L	P	Q	Y	E	F
K	M	R	S	T	U	F

UNIT 7

Section 1
Exercise A
1 generous　2 friendly　3 organised
4 patient　5 optimistic　6 reliable
7 clever　8 honest

Section 2
Exercise A
c

Exercise B
1 Social life　2 Money　3 Health
4 Work　5 Family　6 Health　7 Work
8 Money

Section 3
Exercise A
1 can　2 can　3 can't　4 can't

What's right?
Jeremy can speak Korean.

Exercise B
Ricky can play a sport, speak another language and cook.
Bella can speak another language, but she can't play a sport or cook.

Exercise C
1 Ricky can play tennis.
2 Bella can't play a sport.
3 Can Bella and Ricky speak another language? Yes, they can.
4 Can Bella cook? No, she can't.
5 Can Ricky cook spaghetti? Yes, he can.

Exercise D
1 Marisa and Julia can speak Italian.
2 Can your brother cook Indian food?
3 My best friend can sing and dance the tango. / My best friend can dance the tango and sing.
4 I can read music, but I can't play the piano. / I can play the piano, but I can't read music.
5 She can play tennis, but she can't swim. / She can swim, but she can't play tennis.

What's right?
They can play the guitar.

Section 4
Exercise A
cook: Chinese food, dinner, traditional dishes
play: chess, the guitar, the piano,
drive: a car, to university, to work

Exercise B
1 Chloe can play the piano. She is good at singing.
2 Alicia is good at sports. She likes karate and football. She is good at dancing/salsa.
3 Tony is good at languages. He can speak Russian and German. He can cook Russian food.

Section 5
Exercise A
Adjective	Adverb
slow	slowly
easy	easily
beautiful	beautifully
noisy	noisily
good	well
bad	badly
fast	fast
quiet	quietly

Exercise B
1 He can't swim fast.
2 She can't speak Japanese fluently.
3 She can't play chess very well.
4 He can't talk quietly.
5 He can't read books quickly.
6 They can't ride bikes fast.

Exercise C
1 Dmitri can paint well.
2 Kathy and Sally can run fast.
3 Francesca and Theo can speak Chinese fluently.

What's right?
She can play the piano very well.

Section 6
Exercise A
1 a   2 b   3 b

Exercise B
Conversation 1 ✓
Conversation 3 ✓

Listen and write
Exercise A
1 Sara loves music. She's friendly and generous. She can play the guitar and sing.
2 He's clever and honest. He can speak English and French / play chess. He likes reading and doing quiet activities.
3 She's patient and reliable. She can cook well / make delicious sushi. She likes doing new things.
4 He's athletic. He likes sport and doing exciting things. He can play basketball.

Exercise B
1 H   2 F   3 C   4 D
5 E   6 B   7 A   8 G

Exercise C
Sara likes going to dinner parties / taking salsa classes because she likes music / making friends because she's friendly.
Dominic likes doing crosswords / going fishing because he's clever / quiet.
Brianna likes going to dinner parties / going fishing / doing crosswords because she likes cooking / is patient and likes new things.
Dean likes going snowboarding, visiting archaeological sites / going to concerts because he likes sports and exciting things.

Down Time
Exercise A
nose, sad, honest, sport, hop, on, post, tram, dart, dam, art, smart, map, rose, no, rap, nest, shop, one, made

Exercise B
clever, fast, friendly, honest, patient, organised, optimistic, beautiful

Exercise C
Across:
2 cook   5 play   6 drive
Down:
1 good   3 speak   4 sing

UNIT 8

Section 1
Exercise A
Elena: jacket, skirt (suit), shoes, shirt
Fabio: T-shirt, shirt, jeans, trainers

Section 2
Exercise A
Close to the person speaking:
T-shirt: this, shorts: these, jeans: these
Not close to the person speaking:
T-shirt: that, shorts: those, jeans: those

Exercise B
1 this   2 that   3 those   4 that
5 these   6 those

What's right?
I like these jeans.

Section 3
Exercise A
1 jumper; £29.95
2 shoes; £85
3 T-shirts; £4.50
4 shirt; £19.50

Exercise B
refrigerator: £150
TV: £350
necklace: £1,000

Section 4
Exercise A
1 expensive   2 compact   3 versatile
4 powerful   5 user-friendly

Exercise B
1 versatile   2 expensive
3 user-friendly   4 compact
5 powerful

Section 5
Exercise A
Adjective	Comparative form
small	smaller
clever	more/less clever
big	bigger
happy	happier
compact	more/less compact
up-to-date	more/less up-to-date
cheap	cheaper
old	older
attractive	more/less attractive
popular	more/less popular
exciting	more/less exciting
bad	worse
good	better
pretty	prettier
expensive	more/less expensive
easy	easier
slow	slower
high	higher

Exercise B
1 A games console is less expensive than a laptop.
2 An MP3 player is more up-to-date than a CD player.
3 A digital camera is more compact than a film camera.
4 Emails are cheaper than phone calls.
5 My old computer is bigger than my new computer.
6 Desktop computers are more powerful than laptops.
7 My new mobile phone is less user-friendly than my old one.
8 My new office chair is less comfortable than my old chair.
9 This e-reader is easier to use than that e-reader.
10 His desk is smaller than yours.

What's right?
This computer is better than that one.

Exercise C
1 An electronic dictionary is better than a book dictionary.

2 Our new TV is larger than our old TV.
3 This camera is smaller than my mobile phone.
4 Phone calls on the internet are cheaper than by mobile phone.
5 News on the internet is more up-to-date than the newspaper.
6 My old computer is bigger than my new one.
7 My new tablet is more/less user-friendly than my old one.
8 My laptop is heavier than yours.

Exercise D

1 The laptop computer is more expensive than the desktop computer. / The desktop computer is cheaper than the laptop computer.
2 The dress on the left is smaller than the dress on the right. / The dress on the right is bigger than the dress on the left.
3 The mobile phone on the right is more up-to-date than the mobile phone on the left. / The mobile phone on the left is older than the mobile phone on the right.

Section 6

Exercise A

1 and   2 but   3 or   4 but   5 or   6 and

Exercise B

1 a   2 b   3 b   4 a

Read and write

Exercise A

1 No, she doesn't. The headphones are heavy, and the games aren't up-to-date games.
2 He doesn't need a lot of songs. It's more expensive than the last model.
3 It's more compact than the previous model. It has a bigger screen. It can store more photos and songs, and the internet is faster.

Down time

Exercise A

```
O P E B O S H O T P P R J
T R A I N E R S T U M I A
K S W E J U M P E R T I E
H U H O T K S E R N I J C
A I L I D R E S S E S A C
N T K H R P A T H J H C P
D S B O O T S S W O I K U
B H N E A T H N O E R E R
A S K I R T O O P A T T S
G W D V U J E A N S U I S
K T T R O U S E R S R T H
```

Exercise B

1 cheap   5 attractive
2 compact   6 versatile
3 powerful   7 expensive
4 user-friendly 8 up-to-date

UNIT 9

Section 1

Exercise A

1 peas   2 yoghurt   3 meat
4 watermelon   5 oranges   6 milk
7 bread   8 rice   9 broccoli
10 bananas   11 chicken
12 potatoes   13 cheese

Exercise B

Fruit: bananas, oranges, watermelon
Vegetables: broccoli, peas, potatoes
Carbohydrates: bread, potatoes, rice
Protein: chicken, meat
Dairy products: cheese, milk, yoghurt

Section 2

Exercise A

Countable nouns (singular): apple, banana, tomato, watermelon
Countable nouns (plural): biscuits, crisps, onions, potatoes
Uncountable nouns: bread, butter, meat, milk

Exercise B

1 a; some   3 many; some
2 some/a; much   4 any; some

Exercise C

1 I don't want any cream with my pie.
2 I don't want any vegetables.
3 I want some rice with my fish.
4 How many bananas do we have?
5 Do you have any bread?
6 Do you want a biscuit?

What's right?

I don't drink much milk.

Section 3

Exercise A

1 Hi. Is Janice there?
2 I'm sorry. She's out. Can I take a message?
3 Yes, please. Can you ask her to call me tonight? It's important.
4 Sure. What's your name?
5 It's Alice, and my number is 01568 398431. Thanks!
6 No problem.
The conversation is informal.

Exercise B

1 Could I   4 Could you
2 isn't here   5 Thank you
3 Would you

Exercise C

Possible answer:
Fred: Good afternoon. Could I speak to Helen Stevens, please?
Lily: I'm sorry. She isn't here at the moment. Would you like to leave a message?
Fred: Yes, please. Could you ask her to call me back? My name's Fred Stevens, and my number is 01450 323195.
Lily: Yes, of course.
Fred: Thank you.
Lily: You're welcome.

Section 4

Exercise A

1 to come   2 to have   3 to stay
4 to get   5 order   6 try   7 make
8 to take

What's right?

Let's go to the cinema tonight.

Exercise B

1 d   2 e   3 c   4 a   5 b

Section 5

Exercise A

1 b   2 d   3 a   4 c

Exercise B

1 green salad
2 roast chicken
3 grilled fish
4 vegetable soup

Exercise C

1 Starters
2 Main courses
3 Desserts
4 Beverages

Exercise D

Students should circle: Soup of the day, Grilled fish with potatoes, Coffee
Students should underline: Soup of the day, Roast chicken with vegetables, Cake, Coffee

Exercise E

Lucy's order: £20.39
Dan's order: £15.40
Total: £35.79

Section 6

Exercise A

1 3   2 1   3 2   4 4

Listen and write

Exercise A

Students should circle: spinach, strawberries, nuts, butter, oil, vinegar, paprika, onion

Exercise B

1 Melt the butter over a medium heat.
2 Add the nuts.
3 Cook these for about one minute.
4 Put the spinach, strawberries and nuts in a bowl.
5 Combine the oil, vinegar, paprika and onion.
6 Pour this over the salad.

Down Time

Exercise A

Across: **Down:**
2 products   1 protein
3 vegetables   5 salt
4 drinks   6 fish
6 fruit   7 salad
8 cream

Exercise B

apple tart/pie

UNIT 10

Section 1

Exercise A
Add -ed: explained, played, stayed, watched,
Add -d: decided, liked, lived, prepared, decided
Change y to i and add -ed: carried, married, studied, tried

Exercise B

Base form	Past simple form
do	did
know	knew
go	went
give	gave
get	got
meet	met
speak	spoke
be	was/were
read	read
tell	told

Exercise C
1 went   2 was   3 saw   4 met
5 gave   6 took   7 ate   8 had

What's right?
I wrote you a postcard last week.

Section 2

Exercise A
1 excited   2 boring   3 tired
4 amazing   5 interested

Exercise B
1 tiring; tired
2 exciting; excited
3 boring; bored

Section 3

Exercise A
1 Did; eat; she did
2 Did; eat; he didn't
3 Did; meet; they did
4 Did; watch; they didn't
5 did; do; didn't cook
6 did; do; didn't eat

Exercise B
1 What   3 Did   5 How
2 Where   4 Who   6 Was

What's right?
What did they do at the weekend?

Exercise C
1 c   2 f   3 b   4 d   5 a   6 e

Section 4

Exercise A
1 a   2 c   3 b

Exercise B
1 negative   2 positive   3 positive

Exercise C
1 exam, questions, very hard, failed
2 trip, mountains, snow, slopes
3 match, celebrating, won, two-nil, tickets

Section 5

Exercise A
Possible answer:
From left to right: 4, 2, 1, 3

Exercise B
Possible answer:
Yesterday morning, Frank was on his way to meet some friends when he found a purse on the pavement. First, he looked around to find the owner. Then, he looked inside the purse. He found the name and address of the owner on a driving licence. After that, he went to the address on the licence. The purse belonged to a woman. She was very happy to have her purse back. Finally, the woman gave him a bag of delicious home-made biscuits. Frank was very happy.

Section 6

Exercise A
1 saw   2 took   3 got   4 saw   5 got
6 took

Exercise B
1 e   2 d   3 a   4 f   5 b   6 c

Read and write

Exercise A
Contrast: but
Addition: and
Consequence: so
Sequence: Then, After that

Exercise B
3, 1, 2, 4, 6, 5

Exercise C
1 did
2 I went to a restaurant.
3 Who
4 I went with some friends.
5 What
6 I saw the singer of my favourite band.
7 How
8 I felt nervous but excited.

Down time

Exercise A
1 saw   2 watched   3 liked   4 was
5 carried   6 listened   7 put   8 ate
9 found   10 practised   11 met
12 tried   13 returned

Exercise B
She went to Peru.

Exercise C
1 b   2 c   3 a   4 c   5 b   6 a

Exercise D
amazed, amazing, anything, birthday, bored, boring, cheese, chicken, concert, exciting, famous, fantastic, interested, interesting, music, night, nothing, shopping, show, trip, weekend, what, when, who, yoghurt

UNIT 11

Section 1

Exercise A
1 Chico Mendes; Juliana Rotich
2 Marco Polo
3 Jane Goodall
4 Aung San Suu Kyi
5 Stephen Hawking
6 Aung San Suu Kyi

Section 2

Exercise A
1 When Sam got home, he had a shower.
2 Danuta learnt to speak English when she was four. / Danuta was four when she learnt to speak English.
3 Mike and Patty saw the Opera House when they visited Sydney.
4 When Emi was 16, she went to the USA.
5 Steve started working when he was 21. / Steve was 21 when he started working.
6 Alannah and Kate went backpacking when they were 18. / Alannah and Kate were 18 when they went backpacking.

Exercise B
1 When I saw the crocodile, I screamed. / I screamed when I saw the crocodile.
2 Rosa got her first bicycle when she was 12 years old. / When she was 12 years old, Rosa got her first bicycle.
3 When we went to India, we visited the Taj Mahal. / We visited the Taj Mahal when we went to India.
4 When Gustav graduated from university, his parents gave him a ticket for a trip around the world. / Gustav's parents gave him a ticket for a trip around the world when he graduated from university.
5 Sarah learnt to speak Portuguese when she lived in Brazil. / When she lived in Brazil, Sarah learnt to speak Portuguese.

What's right?
When he was 23 years old, Pietro got married.

Section 3

Exercise A
1 She was born in Lima, Peru.
2 She left school.
3 She got married.
4 She had her daughter Paula.
5 She had her son Nicolás.
6 She moved to Venezuela.
7 She published her first novel.
8 She became a US citizen.

Exercise B
1 When did she leave school? g
2 When did she get married? a
3 When did she become a US citizen? b
4 When did she have her second child? e
5 Where did she grow up? i
6 When was she born? f
7 Where was she born? j
8 When did she move to Venezuela? h
9 When did she have her first child? d
10 When did she publish her first novel? c

Section 4

Exercise A
1 Well
2 Oh, yeah
3 Just a second
4 I'm not sure, but
5 Let me think
6 I can't remember

Section 5

Exercise A
1 her   2 it   3 them   4 us
5 me/us   6 him

Exercise B
1 She bought me the jacket / it for me for my birthday.
2 They gave him the watch / it to him when he retired.
3 I sent her an email / it to her this morning.
4 We showed them the new house / it to them last week.
5 He gave me the book / it to me when I graduated.
6 He bought me some flowers / them for me on our anniversary.

What's right?
She gave him a present.

Section 6

Exercise A

Base form	Past simple form
build	built
win	won
compose	composed
discover	discovered
explore	explored
fight	fought
invent	invented
write	wrote

Exercise B
1 built   2 invented   3 composed
4 discovered   5 won   6 wrote
7 fought   8 explored

Exercise C
1 f   2 h   3 e   4 c   5 a   6 d   7 g
8 b

Listen and write

Exercise A
1 Yes.
2 A biography.
3 They didn't usually get jobs or earn money.

Exercise B
a English author   d to get married
b 1775   e fell in love
c writing   f sad

Exercise C
1 Title and main idea of story; a
2 Main character; b
3 Introduction to story; c
4 Development of storyline; d
5 Change in storyline; e
6 Writer's opinion of film; f

Exercise D

Positive: enjoyable, exciting, fascinating, fast moving, funny, happy, imaginative, scary, unpredictable
Negative: boring, predictable, slow

Down Time

Exercise A
graduated, retired, invented, discovered, composed, wrote

Exercise B
1 the daughter   2 20   3 850

UNIT 12

Section 1

Exercise A
1 F   2 T   3 F   4 T

Exercise B
1 is Pete doing   4 is he meeting
2 is he going   5 Is he playing
3 is he meeting   6 Is he doing

What's right?
Are you going to the cinema tomorrow night?

Exercise C
1 What are you doing tomorrow night?
2 They are watching a football match on Saturday.
3 Is your friend staying at home this weekend?
4 They are eating out in a Chinese restaurant tonight.
5 I am studying for an exam tonight.
6 They are not working here next week.
7 We are visiting my parents tonight.

Section 2

Exercise A
1

Exercise B
holiday, trip, flying, Kenya, adventure

Exercise C
1 To the forests in Kenya.
2 To see wild animals.
3 An adventure trip, exploring unusual and exciting places far away from civilisation.
4 It's tiring and dangerous.

Section 3

Exercise A
1 running   2 dancing   3 horse-riding

Exercise B
1 They are going cycling.
2 They are going shopping.
3 They are going swimming.
4 They are going walking/running.

Section 4

Exercise A
1 am going to improve
2 is going to learn
3 is going to bake
4 aren't going to do
5 aren't going to go out

Exercise B
1 are you going to go
2 are you going to do
3 are you going to go
4 are you going to stay
5 Are you going to study; am
6 Is she going to study; isn't

What's right?
They are going to go out tonight.

Exercise C
1 is going to be a lawyer
2 is going to save money
3 am going to go to China
4 is going to study harder
5 are going to get up earlier
6 are going to go running
7 are going to read magazines in English

Section 5

Exercise A
Toshi: start: bringing a packed lunch to work, drinking green tea; stop: eating junk food, drinking coffee
Pete: start: cycling to work, drinking green tea; stop: eating chocolate, drinking coffee

Exercise B
1 bringing a packed lunch to work; drinking green tea
2 eating chocolate; drinking coffee
3 drinking green tea

Section 6

Exercise A
1 stop spending money on clothes and CDs
2 start saving money
3 buy a video camera
4 take a course in film directing
5 write a film script
6 make a short film
7 enter a film competition

Exercise B
Sergio wants to be a film director. This is his plan. First, he's going to stop spending money on clothes and CDs, and he's going to start saving money. Then, he's going to buy a video camera. After that, he's going to take a course in film directing. Next, he's going to write a film script and make a short film. Finally, he's going to enter a film competition.

Read and write

Exercise B
Consequence: so
Reason: because
Other examples:
I'm going to learn to scuba dive so I can see the coral reef in the Caribbean.
I didn't travel much when I was young because my family preferred holidays in the UK.
Next year, I want to go somewhere far away and very different, so maybe Japan.

Down Time
1 b   2 a   3 c   4 c   5 a   6 c   7 b
8 b   9 b   10 a   11 c   12 b